Folk Music: A Very Short Introduction

Very Short Introductions available now:

ADVERTISING Winston Fletcher
AFRICAN HISTORY
    John Parker and Richard Rathbone
AGNOSTICISM Robin Le Poidevin
AMERICAN POLITICAL PARTIES
    AND ELECTIONS L. Sandy Maisel
THE AMERICAN
    PRESIDENCY Charles O. Jones
ANARCHISM Colin Ward
ANCIENT EGYPT Ian Shaw
ANCIENT PHILOSOPHY Julia Annas
ANCIENT WARFARE
    Harry Sidebottom
ANGLICANISM Mark Chapman
THE ANGLO-SAXON AGE John Blair
ANIMAL RIGHTS David DeGrazia
ANTISEMITISM Steven Beller
THE APOCRYPHAL GOSPELS
    Paul Foster
ARCHAEOLOGY Paul Bahn
ARCHITECTURE Andrew Ballantyne
ARISTOCRACY William Doyle
ARISTOTLE Jonathan Barnes
ART HISTORY Dana Arnold
ART THEORY Cynthia Freeland
ATHEISM Julian Baggini
AUGUSTINE Henry Chadwick
AUTISM Uta Frith
BARTHES Jonathan Culler
BESTSELLERS John Sutherland
THE BIBLE John Riches
BIBLICAL ARCHEOLOGY Eric H. Cline
BIOGRAPHY Hermione Lee
THE BLUES Elijah Wald
THE BOOK OF MORMON
    Terryl Givens
THE BRAIN Michael O'Shea

BRITISH POLITICS Anthony Wright
BUDDHA Michael Carrithers
BUDDHISM Damien Keown
BUDDHIST ETHICS Damien Keown
CAPITALISM James Fulcher
CATHOLICISM Gerald O'Collins
THE CELTS Barry Cunliffe
CHAOS Leonard Smith
CHOICE THEORY Michael Allingham
CHRISTIAN ART Beth Williamson
CHRISTIAN ETHICS D. Stephen Long
CHRISTIANITY Linda Woodhead
CITIZENSHIP Richard Bellamy
CLASSICAL MYTHOLOGY
    Helen Morales
CLASSICS
    Mary Beard and John Henderson
CLAUSEWITZ Michael Howard
THE COLD WAR Robert McMahon
COMMUNISM Leslie Holmes
CONSCIOUSNESS Susan Blackmore
CONTEMPORARY ART
    Julian Stallabrass
CONTINENTAL
    PHILOSOPHY Simon Critchley
COSMOLOGY Peter Coles
THE CRUSADES Christopher Tyerman
CRYPTOGRAPHY
    Fred Piper and Sean Murphy
DADA AND SURREALISM
    David Hopkins
DARWIN Jonathan Howard
THE DEAD SEA SCROLLS
    Timothy Lim
DEMOCRACY Bernard Crick
DESCARTES Tom Sorell
DESERTS Nick Middleton

For more information visit our web site
www.oup.co.uk/general/vsi/

Mark Slobin

FOLK MUSIC

A Very Short Introduction

OXFORD
UNIVERSITY PRESS

OXFORD

UNIVERSITY PRESS

Oxford University Press, Inc., publishes works that further
Oxford University's objective of excellence
in research, scholarship, and education.

Oxford   New York
Auckland   Cape Town   Dar es Salaam   Hong Kong   Karachi
Kuala Lumpur   Madrid   Melbourne   Mexico City   Nairobi
New Delhi   Shanghai   Taipei   Toronto

With offices in
Argentina   Austria   Brazil   Chile   Czech Republic   France   Greece
Guatemala   Hungary   Italy   Japan   Poland   Portugal   Singapore
South Korea   Switzerland   Thailand   Turkey   Ukraine   Vietnam

Copyright © 2011 by Oxford University Press, Inc.

Published by Oxford University Press, Inc.
198 Madison Avenue, New York, NY 10016

www.oup.com

Oxford is a registered trademark of Oxford University Press

Library of Congress Cataloging-in-Publication Data
Slobin, Mark.
Folk music : a very short introduction / Mark Slobin.
p. cm. — (Very short introductions)
Includes bibliographical references and index.
ISBN 978-0-19-539502-0 (pbk.)
1. Folk music—History and criticism. I. Title.
ML3545.S63 2010
781.62—dc22
2010033870

1 3 5 7 9 8 6 4 2

Printed in Great Britain
by Ashford Colour Press Ltd., Gosport, Hants.
on acid-free paper

For Greta and Maya
and all the silenced folk musicians

Contents

List of illustrations

Preface

I began folk music studies in Afghanistan in 1967, as a dissertation topic, and continued by working with the heritage of the eastern European Jews. Having taught folk music topics for nearly forty years at Wesleyan University, I would like to thank all the students, undergraduate and graduate, whose enthusiasm, insights, and research have stimulated my thinking about this fascinating subject. I am grateful to Nancy Toff and Suzanne Ryan at Oxford for involving me in this enjoyable writing project, which I hope is of use both to general readers and to students at various levels, and to Jim Cowdery for a helpful read-through of the manuscript.

The short coverage selectively samples folk music worldwide and covers some of the main issues and perspectives that I see as most salient. I encourage readers to cast their nets widely as they go on fishing in the endless and generous sea of folk music.

Mark Slobin
Middletown, CT
May 2010

Chapter 1
Overview: sound and setting

Locating folk music

This Very Short Introduction will guide and glide the reader
through the main developments and issues of a topic with a simple
name that covers complex layers of meaning and practice. It will
not offer anything like a definition of "folk music," relying instead
on the principle of "we know it when we hear it." Understandings
of the term have varied so widely over space and time that no
single summary sentence can pin it down. The concept behind the
word was born in Euro-America more than two hundred years ago,
and it keeps coming into focus over the generations.

The story begins with the West's enthusiasm for identifying and
analyzing the music of the countryside, and continues worldwide
as modernity engulfs long-standing musicways. In the United
States, "folk music" combines a sense of old songs and tunes with
an imaginary "simpler" lifestyle, featuring the mountaineers of
Appalachia and the African American blues singers, all playing
acoustic instruments—guitar, fiddle, banjo—with a hint of social
significance. Generations reshape and "revive" this model at
any time, including today. In the United Kingdom, "folk" along
these lines blurs into Celtic and regional identities. In Europe,
even though the word comes from the German *volk* (folk), the
genre has different overtones based on local social resonance. For

example, French *musique populaire* and Italian *musica popolare*, each with distinctive meanings, import the English "folk," or "folk revival" to describe some styles. The various Slavic words based on the root term *narod* live in a regional world of their own, with many internal shadings and changing connotations. It is so hard even for Westerners to agree on the term that the International Folk Music Council, which debated long and hard in the 1950s to define its subject, simply gave up and changed its name to the International Council for Traditional Music.

Outside the Western world, "folk" exists as a term from foreign shores. In India, it bears colonial traces and class markings, as *folklorica* does in Latin American usage. Europeans (or, later, Americans) came, observed, recorded, and wrote about the many musical communities they encountered, some of which they labeled "folk," a term that survives and thrives in today's urbanized, organized, and commercialized worlds of music. Sometimes they preferred the word "primitive" in describing the music of small-scale societies, a term that has, thankfully, dropped out of writing today. Musical tradition and innovation continue to flourish—often unlabeled—in the small-scale communities and urban neighborhoods of Africa, Asia, Oceania, Latin America, and the Caribbean and among indigenous peoples in the Americas, Australia, the Arctic, and the Pacific.

One core concept that can help to pinpoint where folk music lives is everyday musical invention. Behind the term lurks the comfortable sense of a face-to-face community that relies on homemade resonance to get through individual and collective experiences. Eventually, in a worldwide ripple effect diffusing from the West, the music moves out into broader public arenas and enters the marketing age. Today and tomorrow, global linkages increasingly bind even the remotest rural music to the cutting-edge scenes of the big cities and little handheld devices and to the boardrooms of corporations and large international organizations.

But don't look for a chronology: this book warns against any straight-line view of musical change. Things loop back, spiral out, and sometimes even repeat themselves. No musician can step in the same cultural flow twice. Yet that musician might travel up or downstream, stand on the rocks in the middle, or jump across them in daring ways. This restless creativity perhaps best defines folk music. Even natural "folk," like the humpback whales, change their favorite songs from year to year. This book will also loop back to selected specific settings, viewing the scene from different perspectives to avoid a partial view of folk music at work.

Locating folk music starts with the word "music" itself. Only a few European languages have a term broad enough to cover all the human sounds that we group together this way. Navajo doesn't, nor does Arabic or most other languages. In fact, including the call to prayer alongside the melodies that mothers sing to their babies, or what singing stars present in nightclubs, can get a researcher in trouble. In most languages, each kind of performed sound might have a separate word, or a whole set of linked terms, without the umbrella term "music," let alone "folk music." So while folk music is clearly "there," it springs from an act of imagination or academic analysis.

Folk music is not a set of songs and tunes; it is more of a working practice. People take available musical *resources* and develop *strategies* to make good use of them. Behind this work lie *aims*, reasons for giving music its share of your life and energy. Ordinary folksingers make music to enhance work with animals and crops, to raise children and keep family ties, to give voice to their beliefs, hopes, and identities, or to signal that they understand their place in society. In traditional Romania or Hungary, a woman was expected to lament loudly and expressively at the funeral of a loved one. She drew on local resources of melody, pitch, dynamics, and text. Her strategy was to conform to the expectations of her family and neighbors, since they would be listening and evaluating her performance, even in such a grief-stricken moment.

A woman's aims might be multiple but certainly would include a strong desire to keep decorum and do things the right way.

Beyond this apparent strategy might lie deeper drives. All around the eastern Mediterranean region, Tullia Magrini states that women project a strong sense of the pain they bear in their social setting, using ritual as a theatrical way to mark stressed moments—healing, death, pilgrimage. These actions can help heal communal scars even as they display women's suffering and power: "In Mediterranean Catholicism and Orthodoxy, human and sacred femininity seem unavoidably bound together in the common destiny of bearing and publicly elaborating the painful sides of life." Folk strategies are often highly gendered in very meaningful ways.

Professional folk musicians have well-known resources and well-honed strategies in their quest to find and please clients. People recognize and value artists who can animate and elevate events. They hire those who have figured out how to match customers' goals with the musician's own aim: to find the most work. More educated musicians and activists—writers, teachers, composers, nationalists, bureaucrats—have a strong investment in their own resources, strategies, and agendas around folk music. Their goals have official backing, in terms of positions, funding, reputation, and access to the media.

Overlapping this social field lies the zone of *aesthetics*, implicit in the villagers' judgment of the woman pouring out her lament. People play favorites with songs, tunes, and musicians. They know what they like, keep it in mind, and value its worth. They hear other people's music and often make it their own, just because of the way it sounds and sticks in the mind. This is the realm of taste, of "I like it that way." Everyone who has collected folk music knows to ask who the best local musicians are and to expect an informed answer. This is a matter of taste, possibly independent of class, gender, or ethnicity. Indeed, it almost seems that one

4

of the reasons humans have music is to sustain a domain of life where taste and memory, technique and emotion, prevail over the normal barriers that divide one group from another.

Of course, *suitability* must be factored in: everything in its season. The need for music to be useful tempers the sheer aesthetic pleasure of performance. David McAllester, who worked with Navajo musicians in Arizona for fifty years, told the story of how he once asked a Navajo if he "liked" a song they were listening to on the car radio. That person could not answer without knowing "what it was good for." But aesthetics and suitability can converge. The Kota people of India say that their ritual music is effective when it is "tasteful to hear," which means that singers should be in synch, have a steady pulse, and carry a strong, nicely ornamented tune for a long period of time.

So the road to folk music knowledge starts with insiders' feelings, which take some time for outsiders to evoke. People may have their reasons for restricting either music itself or conversations around it. The mind-set of the collector can be worlds apart from the thinking of local musicians. Eric Charry cites an interchange in west Africa between Charles Bird, a linguist, and a local interviewee, Diabate. Bird says, "If you help us, we will write down your words and they will live forever." And Diabate replies: "You and your dried words. What are they to me? The meaning of my words is in the moisture of the breath that carries them."

Steven Feld cites a revelatory remark that a member of the Bosavi people made far away in Papua New Guinea. Feld found that his local collaborators had an elaborate system for classifying close to two hundred species of the birds around them, as well as elegant and evocative terminology for the details of bird songs. But when he asked about this, the reply surprised him: "To you, they are birds; to me, they are voices in the forest." Local people understood the bird calls as the sounds of deceased fellow-villagers. To map the insiders' subtle system, Feld had to learn how to talk to them about the larger domain of which folk music is a part: it becomes *expressive culture*, the many ways that people perform feelings and beliefs.

Henry Glassie has eloquently summed up this range of meaningful performance, drawing on his work in the northern Irish village of Ballymenone. Sound itself is highly expressive there, and "the shape of Ballymenone's concept of sound can be imagined as a terraced sequence leading upward from silence to music and from separation to social accord." With each type of heard folklore, "sound becomes more beautiful" and is meant "more clearly to please the listener." This includes "silence, talk, chat, crack [witty dialogue], story, poetry, song, and [instrumental] music." Individual effort aims to "lift people simultaneously toward aesthetic perfection and social union," which begins with the music itself and has a life of its own—it exists and circulates as an acoustic substance that moves into memory and muscle along spatial and neural transmission lines.

When educated Europeans started writing down folk music two hundred years ago, they said the songs were doomed: the old ways will soon be lost, so let's preserve them. This attitude never dies. People keep thinking that as villagers move to the city and as commercial media spreads across the world, folk music will vanish. The famous folklorist Alan Lomax predicted a vast "cultural gray-out." But it hasn't happened. The reason is simple enough: folk music keeps changing and adapting, like so many other aspects of human life, from the family to work to beliefs.

Old-time collectors thought that folk music couldn't survive change because it was fixed, but they were wrong. What they wrote down was not some ancient, permanent "lore," but what the illiterate farmers and peasants happened to be singing at the time. Some of those songs are still with us, but many more have been added over time. True, the cultural environment, technologies, and possibilities keep shifting, not always for good reasons. The folk are driven by drought and desperation to migrate; they are drawn to cities for work, to serve as recruits for wars they didn't start, or simply to get on the road for business or family needs. James Clifford advises us to think of "routes" rather than "roots." He points out that people have always been travelers. Louis Dupree, who roamed the Middle East for decades, once told me that he decided to walk from Turkey to Iran at a leisurely pace, just to see how long it would have taken ideas (and songs) to travel in ancient times. He covered a couple of thousand kilometers (around 1,300 miles) in six months while stopping at campfires to chat with shepherds or hang out in the local bazaar. "See," he said, "it doesn't take that long." Travel and trade have always put music in the backpack and the saddlebag.

When I first went to Afghanistan in 1967, there was really no way I could tell how continuous any of the music I heard was. Nobody had written down or recorded what I listened to in the teahouses of the North. Musicians had few narratives about the past. I would ask them for "old" songs, but sometimes those turned out to be their own arrangements of things they heard on the national radio station, which they had only recently started to receive on the new transistor sets. I simply could not tell what their grandfathers played and their grandmothers sang, and how much that had changed over the generations, since no one had written it up and there were no recordings.

What was clear, though, and remains true, is that at any moment, a folk music system seems layered—at least to an outsider. From the inside, people tend not to think that way. Many common songs have no fixed origin in folk thinking—to take an English-language example, "Twinkle, twinkle little star" is simply a fixed fact in the music culture. How many people know that around 1781, Mozart wrote a theme and variations on the same tune, a French folk song "Ah, vous dirai-je maman," published in 1761. "Twinkle, twinkle" probably takes its tune from this version, along with a text that first appeared in 1806. Such information is hardly relevant to the

English-speaking children of many generations, or to the "amazing Indian three-year-old dancing twinkle twinkle" on YouTube, a young folk performer whose adorable number is likely traceable to English colonialism. Every group has a stock of tunes and texts that have come together so skillfully that they have no past and which expand into an unlimited future.

Overlapping the "old songs" is a second layer of music, items people remember having picked up personally: recent folk music. Folksingers' memoirs, such as the one by the Appalachian singer Jean Ritchie, always detail how they absorbed songs from specific family or community members. In any setting, a beloved uncle stopping over on his way home from a war might introduce a new song that could stick in the mind for a lifetime. In my family, we had multiple melodies for particular sections of the Passover Seder celebration that came from relatives I had never met, but whose strong singing had influenced generations.

Today, advertising jingles and ring-tones quickly become folklorized as part of permanent consciousness. With the current overlap between popular songs and commercial extensions, repertoires have fused and the whole system operates as folk song might have in earlier times. Music-sharing Web sites strongly reinforce this trend by encouraging improvisatory uploading. Yet even though today's Internet music communities can be creative and tightly knit, they are isolated from the pressures of everyday settings, where singers and players mix and mingle on a daily basis within a small physical and acoustic space, whether it is an isolated village or a dense cityscape. In those settings of hardy up-close music-making, a sense of continuity and change might look different to the locals than to the outside visitor. People have their own internal music clocks, depending on their strategies and agendas. They might not want to notice change, or it might be a response to the pressure of intellectual and commercial intervention. Today, folk music is what a child might hear a mother sing, mouth to ear, or it might be digits nestled in computer files, ready to spread around the world, reframed as decipherable, downloadable bits that mostly move into ears through headphones. Many people find no problem with listening to songs without understanding the words, just for the pleasure of the music. Is it still folk music when separated from its physical and social setting? Murray Schafer called that gap between the source and the faraway listener "schizophonia," in order to underline how unnatural it is to listen to distanced music. It would be hard to include schizophonia in any conventional definition of folk music, but even harder to imagine that the site-sound split does not mark most people's listening experience today of music they call folk.

Folk music and the natural world

No matter where and how it is defined or heard, folk music is basically sound waves traveling through the air from a source, into an ear, and then into a brain. Scientists today work hard to figure out how disturbances in the air turn into meaningful music, from the acoustic to the social and personal. Like all music, folk music is naturally made up of four components:

Pitch is the most studied and taught dimension of music in Western societies, from the pitch-centered music notation that children begin with up to the classic "scale-first" studies of scholars. Every note that reaches the ear and is defined by the brain consists of regular vibrations. They pulse through the ear so predictably that we can instantly decipher their "location"—in a fraction of a second—as part of a range of sounds we identify. The standard way to talk about them is "cycles per second" (cps), or "hertz" (hz), honoring Heinrich Hertz, an early physicist. Orchestras around the world usually tune all their instruments from the same standard pitch, A, defined as 440 cps. But all you have to know is that a couple of hundred years earlier, they tuned to 415, or even lower, to understand that pitch is a relative idea, varying locally over time and space as part of deep cultural patterns of listening.

440 is an "absolute" pitch, but most folk music relies more on "relative" pitch, as in early Europe, where each town organist might set his own pitch and tuning system (distances between pitches), depending on factors such as weather or local custom. When I was in Afghanistan, it was clear that no one cared how many cps the local lutes were tuned to, but they wanted the distance between the pitches of the strings to be fixed. Once, a musician-bootmaker named Ghafur Khan put me on display in his shop, as his student. He showed passersby in the bazaar what he had taught me by untuning the two strings on his *dutar*, then having me tune the instrument. It wasn't hard to pick any pitch I liked and just tune the strings to the correct interval, a perfect fourth in Western terms. Of course, the pitch had to be "relatively" accurate, since if it were too high or too low, the instrument would sound sour, and the foreigner would look inept.

Musicians put series of pitches together to make "tunes" or "melodies" in predictable ways according to rules that don't need to be written down—they are self-evident to people who grow up in a particular tonal tradition. Here we move into culture from nature, since what makes a melody is a matter of interpretation and local aesthetics. And it can make people smile, cry, or go off to war.

Duration is about how long pitches last, before they give way to silence or another pitch. This is commonly called "rhythm," but that is more about how the durations are organized into audible and well-known patterns, so again seems more in the domain of culture. Duration gets measured in seconds, but science tells us that it's really milliseconds that count. To grasp what we hear, we need only the tiniest units of sound: half a second or a hundredth of a second can be enough to identify what instrument is playing or even what mood the music is suggesting for the brain to interpret. Durations can indeed cluster into rhythms or "meters," repeating patterns like the one-TWO-three-FOUR of rock 'n' roll or the ONE-two-three of the waltz. But this insistence on fixed duration patterns coexists with much more fluid or very free attitudes toward how to work this component. Citing again the Kota people of India: "Part of learning how to be a musician or a dancer is learning to negotiate the delicate balance of fixed and malleable elements in time." Or, as the Irish writer-musician Ciaran Carson puts it, "One of the beauties of traditional playing is the way a good musician can produce a pulse against the ostensible rhythm of the tune."

What that exactly means might be obvious to some listeners, but enigmatic to others. The closer you come to duration, the more complicated it gets. Time is the basic medium for all folk musicians, and they both flow through it and shape it as they go. Experiments easily show that a listener moving into musical time cannot accurately estimate how much clock-time has elapsed. The variation in estimates is astonishingly wide.

More than pitch, duration gets bodies moving. A huge percentage of folk music is played for dancers. They are often in charge, either by telling musicians *what* to play or *how* to play it. "He who pays the piper picks the tune," the folk say. Dancers are, in some ways, musicians themselves. The thump of feet or the swish of ankle bells can become an integral part of the sound and sense of performance.

Timbre is the least understood of the components: calling it "tone color" is vague at best. Standard music notation doesn't deal with it at all. Timbre arises from the fact that all sounds are not just one pitch, but a cluster of pitches. The brain sorts them out and locates a central focus for practical purposes. But the whole buzzing "envelope" of the other pitches—"overtones," "partials," or "harmonics"—does color the meaning of the pitches. The response can be simply "oh, that's a cello, not a voice" but also "that's a woman," or "that person is sad," or "great guitar sound." Timbre is basic to folk aesthetics and can even lie at the heart of the matter, as among the Tuvans of Siberia, who have what Ted Levin calls a

11

"timbre-centered music," with their intense concentration on the sonic splendor they can coax from their vocal resources as part of their deeply ecological imagination.

Intensity has to do with what's usually called "volume," measured in *decibels* (db). Over a certain number of db, sounds gets painful, as any careless iPod user or anyone walking down a big-city street can testify. Today, unlike all of previous human history, loud and unpleasant sound is actually used as a torture device by armies, a practice that is unbelievably remote from the life of folk music. Several societies make distinctions between indoors and outdoors music based on intensity. Today, even the loudest sounds that acoustic instruments could make seem subdued in comparison to a dance club, but people lived in an entirely different acoustic world—for a million years or more—before the twentieth century. They had another frame of reference for "loud" and "soft."

Folk musicians often keep intensity at one level. A woman singing a ballad doesn't tend to drop to a whisper and then belt out the words of the next verse. A fiddler mobilizing dancers plays at maximum volume to be heard over the feet and conversation, maybe for hours. But there are more subtle ways that intensity comes into play to mark shifts of sections or mood. It automatically alters when an extra instrument kicks into the band mix, raising the volume. Even in the microworld of a two-stringed lute, such as the Afghan *dambura* tunes I collected, the musician's choice to play on one string or on both simultaneously registers as a shift in both timbre and intensity, or he can rap on the lute's soundbox to sharpen the sound and change the sense of rhythm.

None of these four aspects of folk music sound exists in isolation. Testing shows that each is interdependent. Just as timbre changes the sense of intensity, pitch comes across differently depending on duration and timbre. The sense of duration also varies in combination with the other three, and so on. This is why folk music is so aurally rich and satisfying. Music enters the ear as complex sound patterns, then turns into emotion and meaning in the brain. The way this works is currently the subject of a whole new wave of data, analysis, and interpretation on the part of neuroscientists, cognitive psychologists, and ethnomusicologists, from popular books through arcane research reports. Yet almost all the literature starts from European classical and popular music, leaving out the rich folk traditions that could be tapped for understanding these important subjects. A major exception is the work of Judith Becker, who compares people listening to Balinese ritual trance music with "deep-listeners" among the local folk of Ann Arbor, Michigan: Pentecostal Protestants and college students. The results are promising.

Besides brain testing, another way to get at the mental process of music leads through the minds of articulate musicians. Ciaran Carson weaves words deftly to describe what it means to play an Irish dance tune. He can mount a metaphor and take off, as he describes what happens when his band plays a tune called "The Mountain Road." The experience of playing the tune over and over becomes an exhilarating ride: "Each time round we find another nuance, another way of going off the metronome while keeping to the wavy underlying beat, and after so many times you lose count of them...the mountain road winds up and up ornamental gradients, each twist with yet another view; so many zigzags, till you hit the plateau and you see how far this road extends; now you're on a steady rolling level, it's as if the road is taking you, not you taking it...miles of time go by in less time than it takes to tell."

Carson is also very good at describing the simple, functional level of how a musician strikes up a tune. His insistence on metaphors of space, with players choosing trails and forks in the road, suggests the imaging that a folk musician experiences the second he enters the world of a melody: "He organizes time and space within a set of ground rules, and then goes against them subtly when the need arises, for the song has a deep broad structure in

13

which many different mental pathways can be taken." Thought of this way, a tune is a temporary universe of experience and action, with all the natural components, plus social expectations, ready to be reassembled, reshaped, and sent out from the brain and fingers of the musicians to an audience alive with anticipation.

Sound waves and musicians' minds are all part of nature. But the music-environment pairing goes much deeper. Basic studies of the 1980s and 1990s among small-scale societies in a number of regions have yielded fascinating insights into the ecology of music, from the Suyá in the Amazon (Anthony Seeger) to the Temiar in Malaysia (Marina Roseman), from the Kaluli on Papua New Guinea (Steven Feld) to Ted Levin's Tuvan collaborators. In these scattered enclaves of populations, some numbering only in the hundreds, nature is not a neutral entity but an active agent in people's lives, penetrating their dreams and drenching their imagination with the intense resonance of rain forest and mountain biospheres.

For the Temiar, Roseman says that "all personhood, all entities—humans, other animals, plants, mountains, insects—embody bounded souls that can be liberated as unbound spirits. The world resonates with life, with potentially animated being." The Tuvans sing with and about their rivers, mountains, and livestock in ways that push the envelope of what humans can do with their own resonant structures of chest and head cavities. The Kaluli construct songs that take singers and listeners on journeys through familiar local terrain and build them along the lines of the rushing and falling waters of their forests.

These relatively recent accounts build on earlier understandings of how Aboriginal peoples in Australia and Native Americans in North America map, mime, and mine the features of their immediate worlds into songscapes. But more familiar folk can be just as invested in the ecology of sound. Rural Americans and Europeans take seriously the personalities of individual cows or pigs, who recognize and respond to customized songs. The Swiss cast their voices in crafted ways across mountains, and people in the Canary Islands developed a special whistling system to communicate across difficult terrain. As part of "nature," human beings can both take stock of and take part in the sounding of their ecosystems.

Folk music and the social setting

Everyone can sing something sometime. In that sense, there are folksingers everywhere: probably not musically educated in notation but ready to be musical at the right moment. This includes mothers crooning to babies, people singing to animals, or fans chanting football songs in stadiums. In this sense, folk song is intensely egalitarian. But some people don't sing much or well, while others sing often and beautifully. In small-scale communities, from villages to city blocks, people know the really good singers. So even within the democratic system of song, a local song world offers a wide spectrum of possibilities. Age, gender, social group—these and many other factors might also forecast musical patterns. Opportunities run along a range from very open to extremely restricted. In Afghanistan, for example, singing is tightly controlled, limited as to time and place. There is an economy of musical scarcity, based on the local value system. When I was trying to collect music there and found myself frustrated by people's reticence to show off their music skills, I got a letter from a friend working in Java. She said she had a hard time focusing her fieldwork moments, since there was so much music going on all around her—another end of the folk continuum.

Instrumental folk music can parallel or contrast this continuum. In many places, people such as shepherds, with long stretches of time to kill, can make and play local instruments, lending a certain democracy to the literal "playing field." Kids might simply watch people pluck, strum, blow, or drum, and pick it up through imitation. Farther down the spectrum come more specialized musicians. As soon as someone takes a payment from a neighbor to play for an event, he (and it is very often men, not women) becomes something of a professional. Instrumentalists can form an elite corps in many settings, both rural and urban. This is because to play, you have to both get and master an instrument, which involves an expenditure of money, time, and energy that only a few can gather. In the Afghan situation, part of the problem was simply scaring up a lute, even when I had found a musician willing to play. It is a luxury item in a cash-poor economy.

Sometimes, as in the case of Roma (Gypsy) musicians in Europe, the solution is to identify hereditary musician-families who fill the role of folk entertainer more easily than the local majority population can. This could have to do with a widespread feeling scattered across the globe that musicians are a shifty, shady lot, perhaps because they don't do the settled work of agriculture: they may move around and aren't tied into the local linkages of kin and clan. Or, like the Roma and their counterparts in many lands, distrust may arise from being members of offbeat and suspicious social formations. In eastern Europe, this made the Roma useful for country celebrations, since they were in some sense "neuter"—not part of the charged social or sexual politics that surround events like weddings.

People also respect musician-specialists for their special powers, which can be considerable. Among the Mandé people in west Africa, the *jeli* is a member of a hereditary group set apart from society, yet fully integrated. Their control of expressive resources is both wide and deep. Jelis shape and transform events and actions through their words and music, as Eric Charry summarizes: "as performers, jelis specialize in any one of three fields: speech (*kuma*), the vehicle for historical narrative, stories, genealogies, and proverbs; song (*wonkily*) which refers to melodies and lyrics that are unique to named pieces . . . and instrument playing (*foli* or *kasseri*)." And both men and women jelis perform publicly, though differently: "It is primarily men who are considered to be the authoritative guardians of the esoteric knowledge of the jeli and primarily women who deliver major parts of it publicly in performance." Looked at as gendered behavior, the geographic and conceptual distance between Mali, Macedonia, and Afghanistan is huge, but they share common concepts such as the social separation of the professional folk musician and the idea that gender makes a difference in music.

Even deep-seated attitudes can shift very quickly as times change. A new musical instrument can suggest new possibilities. Within a society as small as the Sambla of Burkina Faso, instrumentalists group into clans, with sharp divisions. One group represents older ritual traditions, while the other plays "flashy, complex dance rhythms" on the xylophone, an instrument that entered Sambla life relatively recently. So a musical tool can offer more than just new sonic resources; it can also carve out new social spaces. In fact, across the whole multi-ethnic region where the Sambla live, says Julie Strand, the xylophone has become "a major indicator of cultural identity" for local ethnic groups, defining differences rather than acting as a regional unifying agent.

Instruments create consequences everywhere, as happened with the spread of the accordion in nineteenth-century rural Europe, the guitar's intervention in African music in colonial times, or the sudden influx of fiddles and guitars into rural America when the invention of the mail-order catalog brought instruments to even the most remote locations. As commercial media enter the scene, the figure of the popular singing star can shift the aesthetic, social, and economic dynamics of the music scene. This happened with the invention of the radio musician in Afghanistan in the 1960s, or the African jelis' move into the commercial world-music scene in the 1970s. New media can seriously expand the range of participatory possibilities, even where older folk music worlds keep on functioning.

Part of the process of everyday invention that keeps folk music on the move is the active thinking and talking that shapes how people imagine and create their social soundscape. In any given society, amateurs or professionals may choose to talk about folk music or keep it a tacit understanding. Bernard Lortat-Jacob noticed the difference in researching two Mediterranean musics, contrasting Morocco with Sardinia: "The music of Morocco (at least the mountain music I so loved) could not be commented on; it was played, that is all…what I was to discover in Sardinia,…was a delight in the spoken word and, as far as music, poetry, and dance were concerned, a natural inclination toward the explicit." Some people like to articulate their thoughts about music, and some like to keep quiet. It has nothing to do with the oral or the printed, the "developing" or the "advanced." It is a kind of verbal aesthetic.

Take the 'Are'are people, a very small group on part of one tiny island in Polynesia. Who would think that they are music theorists, especially when they play only tiny sets of panpipes, hollow tubes they blow across? Yet Hugo Zemp made a splash in ethnomusicology thirty years ago by showing that in fact, the 'Are'are love to think about the music they make, with elaborate sets of terms for every little variation in construction and style. On the other hand, in Afghanistan, I found that no one really wanted to go on and on about the music I was collecting. It had low social status, as did the musicians who played it. Long friendship and coaxing, like that undertaken by my Afghan music colleagues John Baily and Lorraine Sakata, elicited some modest analytical talk. But nothing emerged that remotely resembled the discourse of, say, the Javanese, with their multiple, elegant metaphors for ways of playing instruments and building melodies.

A fine example of insider discourse comes from the legendary Irish singer Joe Heaney's exegesis of the *neá* of the Irish folk song. His vivid description emerges from the inside of the system,

the musician's mind, and is not even grasped the same way
by listeners. Heaney said that the *neá* represents "'the sound
of a thousand Irish pipers all through history,' providing both
musical and emotional support." The analysts Sean Williams and
Lillis Ó Laoire explain: It "takes the form of a slightly nasal hum
at the very beginnings and sometimes at the ends of phrases.
The resonant quality produced in the head of the singer, using
the bones of the skull and jaw as resonating bodies, is generally
not perceived by the audience at anything but a nasal tone."
Heaney's description of what it means to ornament an old-time
Irish-language folk song in the *sean-nos* style gives the flash of
insight that only a musician's metaphor can supply: "putting
ornamentations into a song is like when you're courting a girl
with your two arms around her. You're not going to do it the other
fellow's way. You got to do it your own way." Irish folk culture, as
Henry Glassie pointed out earlier, really does value expressive,
elaborate, and eloquent talk.

Outsiders talk about folk music differently. Analyzing folk
music, researchers often apply an X-ray approach. They go for
its bones, the skeletal outline of melodies, tune families, ragas,
modes, rhythmic structures, the way that musical instruments
are built—everything that's a hard surface, able to reflect the
scholar's light and offer a satisfying scientific image. Indeed,
under the amazing surface variation of performances past
and present, live and recorded, lie the bones, just as a crowd
can be reduced to its skeletal similarities under the flesh and
clothing. But you lose a lot if you think of people that way, and
it's the same for music systems. The articulations—ligaments,
tendons, muscles, joints—loom as large as the bones, and the
externals—strong noses, weak chins, powerful torsos, and
all the other features that make individuals stand out—find
parallels in the very distinctive ways that folk musicians gain
local visibility. They do it through the details of performance,
starting with resources and working with strategies of structure
and feeling. Scholars love to nail down specific formulas, but

the overall music system is indeterminate, by its very nature. As Ciaran Carson says about putting over a folk song: "There is no one known way of singing it, since what you knew before will not be what you know tomorrow." Despite the invention of recording, with its forever-fixed versions of songs and tunes, folk music in the long run emerges from everyday invention.

Chapter 2
Close-up: songs, strums, and ceremonies

Now for some actual folk music: three poignant songs that speak directly to people's reasons for singing, from widely separated regions: northern Afghanistan, Jewish eastern Europe, and the Anglo-American world. Each addresses a common complaint of folklife, the sad separation of those who must leave their families and loved ones for the reasons mentioned earlier—work, war, refugee status—the forms of de-territorialization that figure so prominently even today and that still serve as the source for song worldwide. This section introduces some basics of folk song structure, style, and meaning.

A *falak* from Badakhshan, northeastern Afghanistan

I recorded this song from a man named Adinabeg in Faizabad in 1968. Perhaps that is his real name; some people were reluctant to let me know that they were musicians and so gave me other names. Adinabeg, an ethnic Tajik, had come to the major town of the region from a more remote part of Badakhshan, a region bordering Tajikistan, and he sang in the local dialect of Dari, the type of Persian spoken in Afghanistan.

Falak means, literally, the heavens or, metaphorically, fate, against which life is a constant struggle. Adinabeg's references to displacement and nostalgia are only too prophetic of the enormous loss and disjuncture that Afghanistan would undergo, starting ten years later in 1978, with coups, invasions, occupations, dramatic shifts of power, and the uprooting of the majority of the population in and out of refugee camps over the next thirty-plus years.

The text basically stays in the anguished lost-love mode so typical of this genre and familiar in Middle Eastern folk poetry. Displacement is just one of the complaints of the heartsick narrator, who feels rejected by one and all, even though he just wants to be a poor picker of stalks after others reap the harvest of wheat (or love). The agricultural and body language metaphors place Adinabeg's song firmly in a folk music complex of heightened poetic feeling. The mention of the well-known legend of Laili and Majnun (akin to Romeo and Juliet) ties his locale to a broader regional pool of expressive resources. Based on an Arab romance of the seventh century, the best-known version was penned in the twelfth century by the Persian poet Nizami, and the story is known in the folk musics of Arabs, Turks, Persians, Pakistanis, and Indians. Majnun goes mad when he is unable to make Laili his bride, so referencing the tale suggests extreme emotional states of depression. As in so many folk song texts, the first verse is unclear—who is being addressed as "you two?" —is this the singer's rival for his beloved? The way the third verse breaks unexpectedly from monologue to dialogue also reveals folk practice. Often a four-line verse, or quatrain, splits into a 2+2 form. Many of the same structural strategies can be found in, say, the English ballad tradition.

Adinabeg takes this complex and meaningful text, and deepens it dramatically with his voice and instrument, the two-stringed *dambura* lute typical of the region. He starts with a long riff on the lute, setting up an intense rhythm that provides the pulse of the song. Adinabeg uses the full expressive possibilities of what seems to be a "simple" instrument. He puts a finger across the two strings to create a fixed interval that he can move up or down, or he strums a melody on only one string to let the other string create a drone sound. Varying the righthand strokes, he adds to the richness of the rhythmic-timbre configuration of the *falak*, a genre of emotional depth and resonance. The singer's voice, with its long-held, narrow-ranging musical line—he hits a total of only three pitches—contrasts acoustically with the almost percussive *dambura* part. Adinabeg resorts to all the strategies of a sharply honed style of intimate song performance. On the recording (available on the two-disk CD *Afghanistan Untouched*, Traditional Crossroads, 1968/2003, from CDuniverse.com), a buddy starts to drum along but quickly drops out, leaving the solo singer to carry the song, which is meant to be more lyrical than danceable.

The song follows the structure of the text by dividing into four lines separated by instrumental breaks or the dropping-off of long-held notes. But in line four, the way Adinabeg sings sculpts the song structure musically. He starts the line, "yak yâre Aziz guftam, faryâd kunam" ("I say 'dear friend' and cry") but stops after the first three words for some particularly poignant strumming before finishing out the line, ending with a very long note to which he adds a voice break that seems to exhale the inner emotion. Each line concludes with the syllable "ei," not a word but more of a moan. In folk songs everywhere, music faithfully supports words but fills out, enriches, and intensifies their meaning.

In this type of performance, with a soloist covering both vocal and instrumental parts, the musician has complete control of the expressive resources and the range of feeling. Adinabeg balances the text with inflections of the voice timbre, inflects the narrow pitch range through color, and juxtaposes a set of different durations—long vocal line, sharp strumming—with great subtlety. Intensity is not his main focus, the song being set at a fairly constant dynamic level, but the dropping in and out of the voice against the instrument gives this dimension some play as well.

Ex. 1. Adinabeg's *falak* song. Recorded 1968 in Faizabad, Afghanistan, by Mark Slobin

- zar___ zar zar zarzar zār zar zar zar___

(6 times)

You two stay like stars on the roof.
As people, you are like Laili and Majnun.
Once I decided that on your face and head
I would put rouge.

My fried liver is like a yellow apricot.
I am at a loss in a strange place.
I don't get any letters from home.
I say "dear friend" and cry.

Oh my beautiful friend, why do you look so pale?
Either you have given your heart to someone, or are angry.
No, I haven't given my heart to anyone, nor am I angry;
It was God's wish that I become pale.

My girl, may I be your friend.
May I be in a field where there is green wheat.
In this wheatfield, there are many harvesters.
I am a poor man and want to pick stalks.

Folk Music

Adinabeg's *falak* is at once extremely local to its immediate area of Badakhshan, yet resonates regionally in its range of references and universally in its emotional appeal.

A Yiddish song of longing

For one thousand years the Jews of central and eastern Europe developed a large body of folk songs in Yiddish, a blend of various European language components with a Hebrew underlay. These folksingers adapted what they heard among the surrounding Christians to their own aesthetic, religious, and philosophical bent. They took these songs into widespread emigration, from New York to Buenos Aires, from Capetown to Melbourne, where some of them survived the annihilation of the European Jews under the Nazis during the Holocaust. One folklorist, Ruth Rubin, collected a large number of these old songs in North America, and it is from her archive that "Dortn, dortn" comes. Rubin points out the song's similarities to an older German folk song, part of the mixed heritage of the Yiddish folk repertoire.

Not just emigration but also the brutality of the military recruiting policy of the old Russian Empire led to many separations of sweethearts and family members. "Dortn, dortn" expresses a young woman's heartbreak over the delays and distance that keep her from fulfilling her dream of union with her beloved. The text is once again in a four-line stanza, or quatrain, like the Afghan Tajik *falak*. There is a rhyme scheme: the second and fourth lines match, what folklorists call an ABCB pattern, which is extremely common across Europe. Melodically, the song has an ABCD format, that is, none of the four lines of verse-setting repeats the same tune. The internal structure is complex. In the first line, the repeat of "dortn, dortn" seems reflected in the melodic match of the two halves of the line. The melody of the second and third lines each rise to an octave above the opening and closing pitches of the whole song, an "arch" contour, again a very common format in European folk

Ex. 2. "Oy dortn, dortn," Yiddish folksong. Recorded by Ruth Rubin from Ida Smith, 1956. Reproduced in *Yiddish Folksongs from the Ruth Rubin Archive*, edited by Chana Mlotek and Mark Slobin (Detroit: Wayne State University Press, 2007). Courtesy of Wayne State University Press

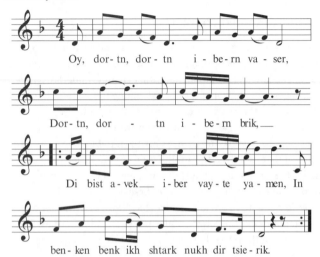

Oy, dor-tn, dor-tn i-be-rn va-ser,

Dor-tn, dor - tn i-be-rn brik, ___

Di bist a-vek ___ i-ber vay-te ya-men, In

ben-ken benk ikh shtark nukh dir tsie-rik.

song genres such as the British ballad. So although "Dortn, dortn" is intensely Jewish in its language and theme, structurally it looks very much like a mainstream European folk song. It would have been sung unaccompanied, by a solo woman, often young, who performed either just for herself or among a group of girlfriends, who might be doing a joint household task such as sewing or preparing chickens for an upcoming holiday feast.

A British ballad of travel and reunion

The ballad is a storytelling song with short verses, most often quatrains, and is a particularly European genre, widespread across the region. Early folk song collectors valued the ballad highly and searched for it tirelessly, sometimes ignoring many other equally important types of folk song. In the late 1800s a Harvard professor,

Francis James Child (1825–96), created such a precise canon of English-language balladry (1882–98) that it crowned the genre's climb to critical approval and even gave his name to the types of songs he published: these are known as the "Child ballads."

Child, like the other great Victorian scholars and fieldworkers, deliberately suppressed songs with erotic, scatological, or other content considered indecent, so the songs are about legendary and historical events, heroes and the mostly tragic fate of love affairs, often among the upper classes. These learned folklorists, stout supporters of the idea of unlettered folk composition, downplayed the fact that many ballads appeared in print in Britain, starting in the 1600s, and circulated freely in both towns and the countryside in various formats. A closer look at folk songs of the 1800s and early 1900s shows a very active movement of songs in and out of print. Sometimes the collectors' own editions worked their way back to the folk for oral revision. So, paradoxically, print can keep oral tradition alive and vital. Sound recordings, beginning in the early 1900s, just add another channel to the mix. The reason that "Barbara Allen," the most collected ballad, is so much more popular in the United States than in the British Isles might have to do with its frequent publication in American songbooks.

The nineteenth-century scholars got caught up in a long argument about whether songs emerge from collective composition or come from individual invention. That seems like a pointless quarrel today because individual and collective efforts coincide. The folk recognize the contributions that particularly talented people make to collective enjoyment and memory. But they condense those scattered efforts to form a communal pool of expressive resources and strategies. It's all in the service of group agendas about when, where, how, and why to sing and play their music.

Child 53, "Young Beichan," falls into this category of complex circulation. Also known as "Lord Bateman," "Lord Bakeman," or "Lord Beicham," it was very popular in both Britain and North

America. The song tells the tale of an aristocrat who takes a sea voyage abroad, only to find himself captured by the Turks or some other "heathen" enemies and painfully imprisoned. The jailer's (or prince's) daughter takes pity on the lord and sets him free; grateful, he promises to marry her. Back home, time passes, and the lord sets a wedding day for a local bride. Just then his rescuer, sometimes called Susie Pye, turns up at the lord's gate. He honors his vow to the foreign woman and sends his jilted bride on her way luxuriously: "she came to me with a horse and saddle / She may go home in a coach and three [horses]."

This open-minded, happy ending for a song of separation stands out among the more bloody confrontations, such as the upper-class love triangle in Child 73, "Lord Thomas and Fair Eleanor." There, Fair Eleanor, rejected by Lord Thomas, confronts his bride, the nut-brown girl, who stabs Fair Eleanor, leading Lord Thomas to "cut off her head and kick it against the wall" and to end the tale by falling on his own sword as a suicide. Child disliked sex but had nothing against violence. These dramatic scenes have drawn many singers to the ballads throughout the years. The British folk star Kate Rusby says she loves them for "the stories and the simplicity...they're like mini-films," and they are indeed often cinematic, seeming to tell the story in discrete shots and countershots like a movie.

Examples 3 and 4 give two Scottish tunes for "Young Beichan," one from the singing of Thomas Moran, from Ireland, and the other from the influential singer Jeannie Robertson, of Scotland. Both versions feature the pentatonic pitch organization particularly common in Scotland, which means you can play the tune on just the black keys of the piano, adding up to five notes to the octave. Both versions have a repetitive melodic structure for the four lines of the text's verses. Moran crafts the melody into two very similar lines, one for the first two lines of text and the second for the other half of the quatrain. The two halves differ at the end, the first landing on the note E and the second on G. Robertson moves the melody around, twisting the pentatonic tune like a kaleidoscope by using the same components to form a different picture, but keeps to the two-part structure, with the same endings on E and G.

To the ear, as opposed to this black-and-white notation, the two versions are much less like each other—this is a good case of the flesh being different from the bones of folk music. Moran seems more staid. Robertson's fame and influence stem partly from her extraordinarily expressive and expansive way of singing. She combines precise placement of pitches and turns of melody around certain notes with an emotional charge lacking in a more straightforward style such as Moran's. But both singers stick to an overall concept of the song that offers unity under the surface differences. Each divides the tune into two parts, with the A-B unit built like the C-D unit, except for the different endings. And the two share a sense of tonality that relies on five notes to the octave, what scholars call an anhemitonic (without half steps) pentatonic modality, which is common worldwide in many folk music traditions from Scotland to China.

Moran sings in a free style attuned to speaking the text, with pauses after lines. You can feel a "pulse" behind the singing, but you can't exactly tap your foot to it—there's that inner sense of a patterned duration, which gives folk performances both meaning and style. The standard notation (shown in exs. 3 and 4) gives little sense of either singer's flexibility, since eighth notes, quarter notes, and the rest measure only time-units in multiples of two, while folksingers think elastically. It's like using a rubber band instead of a stapler to hold something together. As with so many folksingers, Moran also builds a musical line that is not exactly expressing the words, for example when he stresses the unimportant word "and" that connects the third and fourth lines of text (marked A, B, C, D in the transcription example), or stresses "ready" on the second syllable. The "and," like the "O" that starts the first three lines, builds melody more than meaning.

Likewise, Robertson makes two syllables out of the word "door," with the stress toward the end, and echoes this move with the way she handles the word "small" in line C, another unimportant one-syllable word. These stylistic graces allow Robertson to make melody do more expressive work than text in shaping the listener's experience of the song.

Left unclear is who is speaking about "our" door and being so amazed at the amount of heavy gold belted around the "prettiest lady I've ever seen." Description gives way to social commentary as the observer notes that there's enough value there "to set Northumberland free," although the narrator does not specify the historical moment—when and where is this taking place? Why does a Scots singer—the word "muckle" gives away the dialect—care about neighboring English Northumberland? These and many other such questions have made the British ballad the topic of endless analysis by scholars since the eighteenth century.

In terms of performance style, worth noting is the way Moran stumbles a bit at the song's opening before settling down into his accustomed groove, starting around a B-flat that is not in the eventual pentatonic. This is very common on folk song recordings. When fieldworkers ask folksingers to sing, quite out of context—how often do the "informants" find themselves in front of a microphone, while perhaps not feeling at all like singing?—it takes even seasoned singers a while to find their musical footing. A closer look at Jeannie Robertson's climb to folk song stardom reveals that when first "discovered" by the Scottish scholar Hamish Henderson, she was in no mood to perform, being worn out from taking care of her sister's children. Nevertheless, she sang for hours, being hospitable as many such singers can be, allowing Henderson to "discover" her. Robertson belonged to a social group usually called "Travelers" in Scotland, of uncertain origin and often discriminated against, yet she became an exemplar of the Scottish song, showing once again how outsiders can sustain and restore local folk music traditions.

Ex. 3. Thomas Moran's version of "Lord Beicham" (Child 53). Transcribed by Mark Slobin from *The Child Ballads I*, Topic 12T160

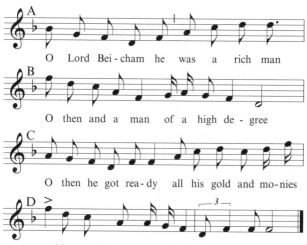

O Lord Bei-cham he was a rich man

O then and a man of a high de-gree

O then he got rea-dy all his gold and mo-nies

and he vowed strange coun-te-ries he would go see.

O Lord Bacon, he was a rich man
O then and a man of a high degree
O then he got ready then all his gold and moneys and
He vowed strange counteries he would see.

O and he sailed east and he sailed west
Until he sailed into Cumberlands
And he was taken by a hethen king
By a hethen king o Lord Bacon was.

He bored a hole all through his right shoulder and
He bound him up to the oak so strong
He bound him up to the oak so strong
Until of his life he was quite weary.

It happened to be upon a holiday
When the king's fair daughter was passing by
And as she looked in on the prisoner's window
Twas on Lord Bacon she cast her eye.

Ex. 4. Jeannie Robertson's version of "Lord Beicham." Transcribed by Mark Slobin from *The Child Ballads I*, Topic 12T160

There is a lady at our hall door

She's the prettiest lady I've ever seen

She's as muckle gold around her meddle small

That would buy Northumberland and set it free.

I'll bet you one pound against a penny

It's my young Susan Pye from across the sea

For it's you come here on a horse and saddle

I'll put you back by a coach and three.

Looking at these English-language storytelling songs transatlantically makes it easy to see the folksingers as mobile musicians. Songs shift shape when they get on ships and planes. Tristram Coffin and Roger Renwick point out that "the most obvious sort of ballad change centers about the simple alteration of words and phrases," so that in American versions of Child 243, "the place to which James Harris asks the carpenter's wife to go varies from Sweet Willie, sweet tralee and Tennessee to Italy, the deep blue sea, and calvaree." The "burial in the choir" becomes "burial in Ohio." Many forces are at work here: singers localize songs simply to place the action nearby, rather than in some "foreign land." Other changes crop up from mishearing or memory lapses. No single explanation can covers the full range of change that even a single song can undergo as it moves from place to place or across generations.

The three songs we've studied do not represent some older folk music sensibility. The topic of the pain of separation stays steadily salient, as related in Carol Silverman's recent report of Balkan Roma (Gypsy) communities living in the United States. New Yorkers can also lament having to leave their loved ones to eke out a living: "Working abroad is very hard / Listen to me my friend / You are without yours (your family) / Your heart is burning," or "The life working abroad / Is very difficult, Roma / Day and night you work / For coffee and bread." Similar sentiments resonate throughout the vibrant music of the men who pull up roots to do desperately dangerous work in the South African mines: "labor migration...is one of the most powerful forces shaping Black South African life, music, and performance," states Carol Muller. Migrating musicians leave their families behind but bring along their spirit and their music.

The sung solidarity of either migrants or villagers can bring people together into moments of powerful collective performance. The line between individual and group singing is often blurry. Someone can lead a collective song, everyone can sing one line together, or they may break into groups with separate melody lines, in which case it's called polyphony. In Bosnia, some villagers carry on the tradition of *ganga*, which brings together small groups of young women or men who may have grown up singing together, so they tune in subtly to each other's sense of line and collaboration. Traditionally, a girl marrying out to another village might have a hard time joining a *ganga* group, since the style of vocalization is so intensely local. Groups stand shoulder to shoulder and work on their singing, and then can appear informally at public events—perhaps a country fair—to show off their sound and their proud presence. When the ethnomusicologist Ankica Petrović first brought singers to the radio station for a recording, the women rejected the sound engineers' plan to place a microphone in front of each singer. Knowing very well how their resonance carries, they told the technicians where to place a single mic for optimal sound.

Ganga songs start with a solo, then move to a tight, precise, exquisitely controlled collective section, with pitches that can be hair-raisingly close together. Singers have a precise vocabulary for how the music should sound: *dobro slozene*, "well put together," for the fit of the voices, strong dynamics, protracted sounds, and a variety of *okretaje*, melodic patterns. Overall, the effect should display *veliko umijece*, or exceptional artistry, a phrase they also use for the construction of everyday objects, such as carpets, stockings, or storage bags. This carryover of a descriptive term reveals an underlying folk aesthetic that crosses domains of experience and invention. At the same time, *ganga* should be *zabava*, entertainment, marking it off from stockings and carpets. So music needs to be both well crafted and affective.

Ankica Petrović says that "ganga singers are usually boon companions and are well thought of in their society because joy is treated as a very welcome emotion." The singers themselves fall into a trancelike state while singing. Good performances can move listeners to "tears and 'shudders,' but with a sense of happiness. They arouse feelings of love and sexual passion among younger people, as well as strong feelings of regional identity among both young and old alike." In this way, collective singing can project the inner unity and strong emotion of the singers across the entire community: folk song at its most powerful.

Somewhat surprisingly, Tony Seeger describes a similar situation among folksingers culturally, socially, geographically, and historically as far from Bosnia as you can get: the sparse Suya people of the Amazon rain forest in Brazil. He relates an evening when boys learn new songs from their fathers or other relatives, in the men's house: "everyone listens, laughs and jokes. The village is in that desirable state of collective euphoria...that should be the part of any ceremony. When people feel euphoric, they are happy and want to sing. Singing makes them happy." Seeger's suggestion of the circularity between happiness and singing seems particularly salient. For not only are individual brains being stimulated by sounds to help generate happiness, but the social meaning of the songs as collective effort enables this transformation.

Seeger finds it hard to locate "music" within the broad range of expressive vocal production of this very small group. This is partly because he identifies "a kind of continuum" from chanted and sung words, close to everyday speech, to ancient, unknowable texts, performed in ceremonies where the singers "undergo a metamorphosis in which they became a kind of being that was both human and mouse." And "it is hard for an anthropologist to get translations directly" from the source of songs: "jaguars, birds, bees, and extinct enemies." Here the sense of a "collective" goes beyond the visible community of the village, spiraling out in time, space, and species to an enormous cast of characters.

The mutability of music flows in harmony with this idea of transformation. In many folk settings, group singing marks moments of human transition. Unfortunately, this power of the communal voices can draw the attention of the people in power, who control the lives of the folk. This was the case of "keening" in Ireland, a form of women's group lament around death and burial rites. In modern times, and for the British authorities who ruled Ireland for so long, keening "came to be seen...as a symbol of the incorrigibility of the Irish, representing their recalcitrant resistance to civilization and domestication...a prominent sign of Irish wildness and savagery." It also became part of the tourist circuit of the colonial powers as they searched for the shock of the exotic in nearby Ireland. But for the Irish themselves, the emotional force of the lament stayed strong, a collective symbol of group feeling in a situation where outright resistance was not possible.

Besides the song, another format of folk music springs from everyday invention and channels collective energy: the dance tune. Very few studies actually correlate the way musicians and dancers work together to drive bodies and spirits into celebration of a communal moment. The cooperation can be an exchange of cues and ideas, or one side can take charge of the action. For the Sambla of Burkina Faso, with their outstanding xylophone skills, songs share social space with dance music.

At a celebration, "nearly every adult present has a song associated with them, allowing the soloist to call their attention at any time"

1. Members of the Diabate family in Konkolikan village, Burkina Faso, playing music for local dancing among the Sambla people.

by playing it; "at that point the person is obliged to ... dance to the song" and interact "verbally in short exchanges with the soloist, to which he responds musically on the instrument," a collaboration that ends when the honoree drops small bills one by one on the instrument in payment for the praise. Everyone watches, and could potentially take a turn, a social strategy that subtly inflects the individual-collective interaction through music and dance.

A dance tune of the Afghan Uzbeks

Dance contexts evoke a fluid, fascinating interactive mix of skills and enthusiasm. Tunes are often built out of short sections that repeat, allowing for a quick overview of how variation unfolds within and between performances: the spotlight is on inventiveness.

One example from the wide world of the dance tune will stand in for very widespread patterns of the craft of instrumentalists. The Uzbeks are a Turkic people who mostly live in Uzbekistan, with a branch in neighboring northern Afghanistan. There, they play dance tunes that ring out in the teahouses of scattered towns or at private parties inside walled mud-brick compounds. Although the Uzbeks and their neighbors, the Persian-speaking Tajiks, share some musical ideas and instruments, everyone feels that certain tunes (*naghma*)—are more Uzbek than others. One favorite that I collected most during the peaceful era of the 1960s had no name. I had to sing or play it to get musicians to perform it. On my Web site, http://afghanistan.wesleyan.edu (under Ethnic Subcultures/ Uzbek), there's a sample of six versions. Folk music scholars love to pile up "variants," such as the versions cited earlier of a single English ballad. The idea is to get the big picture of everyday invention through the single lens of an individual item. The first and last of those examples on the Web site appear as numbers 1 and 3 in example 5 (see page 43), as performed by two of the main musicians of the region at the

2. Snapshot of local dancing by the Polish ethnographer Jozef Obrebski, who photographed folklife in Ukraine's Polesie region in the 1930s.

time, Bâbâ Qerân and Bangecha Tashqurghâní. My notation here makes the case that no matter who's playing the tune, it has three well-defined sections labeled A, B, and C. It's a way of generalizing across very different styles of performance by a number of musicians widely separated from each other.

The instrument of choice is the *dambura*—a long-necked, two-stringed lute with no frets—that local Uzbeks and Tajiks share. It doesn't match any of the many other long-necked lutes of the greater Afghan-Central Asian-Middle East region. In the *falak* song (ex. 1), the Tajik Adinabeg deployed the modest resource of the *dambura* creatively, but he didn't exhaust its possibilities. The musicians of example 5, on the other hand, like to play only one string at a time or use one as a drone: a string you don't put your finger on, so that it just sounds the same pitch all the time. Adinabeg has the mountain Tajik preference for making the upper string a drone, whereas Uzbeks prefer the lower string to do that job. He might place one

40

3. Village musicians, featuring the ever more popular accordion, in the Polesie region of Ukraine, 1930s.

finger across both strings (making a parallel fourth), which Uzbeks never do. So while sharing the *dambura*, an instrument not favored by their neighbors, the Uzbeks and Tajiks find ways to separate their sounds. It's a fine lesson in the interaction of shared and distinctive approaches to folk instrumental music by two ethnic groups.

Listening to the six variants on the Web site, or looking at the four printed versions here, offers a good chance to hear intense individual and local variation within the microcosm of a small soundworld, one that was at the time extremely isolated from the world-music system. The top two versions of example 5 are both from Bâbâ Qerân. That elderly gentleman figured as the dean of the *dambura*; he was about seventy at the time, considered a ripe old age. One of the reasons people said they valued his playing was because he had a rock-steady beat. Remarkably, his two versions are identically paced, although I recorded them one year apart. His name is really a nickname: *Bâbâ* is a word for an old guy, and *qerân* was the smallest unit of Afghan currency, half a penny. It was attached to his name because

4. Father and son instrument-makers building a *dambura* in their rural workshop in northern Afghanistan, 1968.

"wherever there's a *qerân*, he'll play," a strong folk statement about the tenuous and tenacious life of the local minstrel. This folk epithet speaks eloquently to the state of local musicians in an economy of true scarcity, a "zero-sum" situation, where any *qerân* a man can earn, taken from someone's pocket, is sheer gain, since there was very little money in circulation. I never found out his original name.

The bottom two variants of the Afghan Uzbek dance tune come from one of the finest regional musicians, Bangecha Tashqurghâní. He became a victim of liquidations during the first wave of invasions, occupations, uprisings, and civil wars that marked Afghanistan's descent in chaos and violence. His first version, the third entry in example 5, displays the off-the-beat opening he did only once in the performance, since it is so distinctive and shows another way to play the first section of the *naghma*. As the fourth entry shows, even the same musician can play a single tune in very different ways, deploying the modest variability that the two-stringed *dambura* offers to maximum effect. But notations

Ex. 5. Afghan Uzbek *naghma* dance tune, variant versions: 1 and 2 by Bâbâ Qerân, 3 and 4 by Bangecha Tashqurghâni. Fieldtapes of Mark Slobin, 1967–68

such as these can only capture a skeletal X-ray of the live sound, not the whole flesh-and-blood performance. Absent are Bangecha's wonderful mouth sound effects and the rhythm he so markedly musters to make this not just a melody but a danceable tune for an appreciative male audience. Bangecha even had a little dancing dog to liven up his act.

In some ways, the everyday experience of known folk musicians like Bâbâ Qerân and Bangecha—a kind of recognized, if sometimes distrusted, performing elite—shows broad similarities in many parts of the world. They have to please patrons, stock up on tunes, gauge audience response, and satisfy their own tastes and heritage. They are working members of a local, but also worldwide, clan of performers. Professionals follow often exquisitely detailed, often implicit rules that regulate how far they can go in pushing the envelope, both socially and musically. They are at once conservatives and experimentalists, curators and dismantlers of the traditions in which they work. At some point, probably just before I met him, Bâbâ Qerân had to figure out how to add popular tunes from Radio Afghanistan to his regular repertoire, since people were now listening to songs, often in another language, from a faraway studio orchestra. City songs were being played on other instruments, such as the *tanbur* and *rubab*, by urban musicians. The resulting medleys that Bâbâ Qerân developed, weaving older and newer, ethnic and national melodies can serve as a metaphor for musicianship, a way of both embodying and expanding the folk music system.

The social space of ritual

Beyond the solace and sentiment of folk song or the animation of the dance tune lies the domain of ceremony and ritual. Ritual both defines a specific moment and opens up a wider social space. It can be incredibly conservative or contain seemingly contradictory messages. Suzel Reilly describes how the singing of Christmas processions of *folia* groups in southeast Brazil combines religious faith with working-class solidarity: "Their links to one another become defined by their common devotion to the Magi [the Three Kings], whose voices temporarily fill the gaps between them, and for a fleeting moment devotees can feel as though they are resonating in sympathy with a perfectly tuned universe." But just as they affirm a divine moral order, the singers and musicians implicitly sound a statement about their intolerable social situation. They "express their aspirations" and "equip themselves for their constant struggle to preserve their dignity within a wider social sphere marked by tenacious boundaries and thinly veiled forms of racial discrimination."

In many folk music settings, weddings stand out as major ritual events that feature layered expression, individual and communal, and are often remarkably fixed in form. As one Hungarian source says, weddings accumulate "ceremonies containing mythical, religious-ritual, legal, economic, musical, and mimic elements. In some places they become almost festive plays with their chief and supporting characters, supernumeraries, fixed scene, time, music, dances, and audience." Such was the case of many a Russian wedding scene, which continued in full force even in Soviet times (1917–91) in remote outposts of the far-flung countryside. Today, people are bringing back many old customs of this sort.

A short summary of the extremely complex wedding ceremony in the village of Varzuga, near the Arctic Circle on the White Sea, can stand in for a host of wedding frameworks worldwide. The Varzuga wedding consists of eleven different stages, with numerous small substages and ceremonies, most of which have their own set of songs. This large, ritual set-piece differs from the cycle of events just down the road in neighboring villages. The molten energy of everyday invention can freeze into regularized rituals. This fixity helps to smooth over any tensions that might arise between two proud families now joining into a tight connection, with possibly far-reaching consequences for alliance or feuding.

Here is a thumbnail sketch of the eleven scenes of this social drama, as collected in the 1960s by Russian researchers from older women of the Varzuga village:

Matchmaking. The matchmaker steps into the family hut of the prospective bride, but not beyond the doorway beam, seeking permission. If granted, he proposes a match in highly stylized phrases. If the family rejects the match, they smear his head with flour.

Handshaking. Once the deal is struck between the families, especially the amount of the dowry that goes to the groom's side, the wedding cycle officially begins with a lighting of the lamp that hangs by the family icon, a sacred painting. The bride moves to a designated spot and starts up a long, showy process of formulaic lamenting, bemoaning the moment when she has to leave her family home and fall under the power of the groom's kin, notably her new mother-in-law.

Girlfriends' visits. The next day is full of song, as the maiden's girlfriends gather at her hut to lend moral support. Sewing clothes for the trousseau, the girls (all aged about fifteen) sing a song cycle about the impending marriage. Analyzing one song from this set, "Na solnechnom vskhode," can give a sense of how a rigidly stylized repertoire operates. The song is in a leader-chorus format, typical of many eastern European genres. The responding voices break briefly into two lines, creating polyphony, very common in eastern and southern Slavic singing, such as the Bosnian *ganga* cited earlier. The girls sing in an expressionless style, with a circular, nonstop quality of singing. There are no clear line breaks. This detached manner underlines and expresses the ritual nature of the song as if the singers are expressing: it's not us in particular, but the village as a whole, indeed, the tradition that is singing. Just as ritual dance and action emerge from behind masks in many parts of the world, so singers seem to put a mask on their voices for such songs.

The scale structure of "Na solnechnom vskhode" is worth a closer look. There are basically only four pitches, D, G, A, and B-flat in this transcribed version. This pitch-set occurs not just in these Varzuga wedding songs but also in a huge number of other older melodies in the Russian tradition that relate to rituals of the summer season. So the tonal content represents the intersection of the individual life cycle of this particular girl with the yearly cycle, so important in rural agricultural life. Again, these folk keep individuality to an absolute minimum. Like other songs in this wedding repertoire, "Na solnechnom vskhode" varies only in one detail as sung from maiden to maiden: the name of the current bride and groom, which slide in to a standardized slot.

Bathing. The girlfriends lead the bride to the public bathhouse. At the door, she sings a special lament on an improvised text, repeated after the bath, a rare moment of individuality set into a communal framework.

Gifts and unbraiding. Sitting in a special place, in a new outfit, the bride watches stylized gift-bearing and listens to farewell formulas from her female kinfolk and girlfriends. A professional female lamenter helps the bride wail and sings songs targeted at each type of guest—godparents, siblings, and so on. Finally, a sister unbraids the girl's maiden plaits, later to be redone into the married woman's knots under a kerchief. Peasant life marks transformations physically as well as musically.

Greeting. Seated in another special place, the bride receives non-kin guests. Villagers flock to the porch to look into the hut and listen to the songs.

Blessing. The groom and his party can arrive only after the bride's parents offer a formal blessing in a solemn and emotional moment.

Ex. 6. Northern Russian wedding song, "Na solnechnom ugreve."
D. M. Balashov and Lu Kraskovskaia, eds., *Russkie svadebnye pesni*
Terskogo berega Belogo moria **(Muzyka, 1969)**

Na sol-nech-nom-y vskho-de, na u-

gre - ve __ da sto-it be-la-ia be-

ryo - za ku-dy-re -

va - ta, da mi-mo

[last verse only]

(prozdrav-) lia-em A-le - ksan-dro-vich's Mi-

khai - lo-vy-noi!

At dawn, at the warming / A bushy, white birch-tree stands.
Past that white bushy birch-tree / Goes no road, no path
No broad way, no footpath, no passageway.
Gray geese fly, but do not honk / White swans fly, but do not cry.
Just one young nightingale sings.
He flies to the father's courtyard / To the mother's high tower.
He gives Annushka heartache / Makes it known to Mikhailovna
That Annechka shouldn't be living at her father's / Singing in the
    high tower
Nor combing her unruly head / Nor plaiting her blonde braid
Nor twining a ribbon into her braid / Nor wearing a red-gold belt,
But that Anna should be with Ivan / To be (his) father's slave,
To be mother's daughter-in-law / To be Ivan's bride.
So hail to Ivan and Anna! Let's congratulate Alexandrovich and
    Mikhailovna.

Groom's arrival. The groom's party arrives via a prescribed route.
Everyone is precisely seated. The bride and bridegroom are now
"prince" and "princess," and relatives are "lords and ladies," who
sing choral songs until the bride, led by her father, comes in with
a tray of small vodka glasses. She offers them in strict order to the
groom's kinfolk, then she exits to be dressed. This whole scene is
accompanied by songs in a unified style. Should anything be done
in the least bit improperly, the villagers will blame future marital
troubles on this carelessness.

Church ceremony. So far, organized religion has no part in the
wedding ritual. But now everyone proceeds to the village church,
with the local priest leading hymns, followed by a brief Russian
Orthodox Christian ceremony.

Viewing and banquet table. Now the action shifts to the
groom's house. People rearrange the bride's hair and finally feed
the bride and groom, and both sides of the wedding party sit in
prescribed order as they begin full-scale feasting and singing. A
chorus chooses different song for each type of guest—parents,

relatives, friends, bachelors, old folks—demanding payment for this service. Cries of *gor'ko, gor'ko!* ("bitter") ring out, each one requiring a drink. Eventually, the guests join the singing, and dancing starts up for everyone but the bride. As the party breaks up, the couple accompanies the bride's parents halfway home on a specially decorated reindeer, since this is Arctic country.

Final stages. The next morning, the bride starts married life by getting up early and helping her mother-in-law make pancakes for a ritual dinner for all the kinfolk. One last feast and final gifts end the wedding, completing weeks of elaborate and expansive preparation and days of carefully observed ritual. If all goes well, the families have avoided clashes and grievances, everyone has been sufficiently respected, and the couple have the proper platform for a good marriage.

By the time the Russian researchers documented the Varzuga cycle, only the songs remained. Modern couples were unlikely to undergo this type of transformation into married life. But already in the 1970s, urban enthusiasts began to go out from major Russian cities into the countryside to learn the old customs in a personal way, even getting married in a village in order to pick up pointers. Dmitry Pokrovsky's ensemble, under the watchful eyes of Soviet censorship, put out recordings and ended up touring internationally with their trove of village versions of folk songs. After the end of the Soviet Union in 1991, the ascendancy of Orthodox observance, new national consciousness, and an urge for roots have led to considerable revival of older folk music. Everyday invention continues in our times as a new "folk" looks back for the future.

Chapter 3
Intellectual intervention

The folk themselves do not tend to study, analyze, and publish their musical folkways. Why did the intelligentsia—the educated elite of thinkers, scholars, artists, and upper-class amateurs—take on this task by intervening in the everyday experience of what they defined as "the folk?" The variety of this list of activists signals the mixed motivations and crossed networks of an ill-assorted group. Only in the early nineteenth century could romantic artists coincide with upper-crust aristocrats and bourgeois dabblers, or have much to do with pedantic scholars. It all has to do with two main trends of the emerging modern world—identity-seeking and institution-building, and two agendas—the nationalist and the universalist.

Modern life disrupted and reorganized Euro-American life. Industrialization brought a shift to the cities, made peasants into proletarians, and raised the bourgeoisie above the aristocrats. The small, educated, and artistic elite scrambled to find new identities. In 1724, Allan Ramsay, a wig-maker turned writer, put out his quaintly named *Tea-Table Miscellany*, a goulash of folk songs and his own work, meant to be read aloud as the elite of Scotland gathered for tea and conversation. By 1765, the title of Thomas Percy's *Reliques of Ancient English Poetry* cast the folk song as a picturesque and affecting remnant of the good old days. On the Continent, the search for new identity was perhaps more urgent, as Napoleon swept away the old social order. Often, the personal combined with collectives that ranged from the utopian to the political. Particularly the Germans, fragmented into dozens of little states until 1860, needed a common purpose in their quest for unity, to be founded on the *volk*, a complex compound of sentiments and semantics. Nationalists across Europe eagerly touted folk music as the "spirit" of that hard-to-define concept the "nation."

As the 1800s advanced, science, technology, and nation-states enforced rational forms of control. But a pushback of the passions drove thinkers, artists, and collectors to consider the countryside as an alternative space of feeling, a place to look for personal and group grounding in turbulent times. The remaining preserves of peasantry and village life offered an arena of intellectual and artistic play. Composers whipped out their notebooks to catch local tunes they could weave into their works. Scholars searched for the origins of modern languages in antique song texts, and writers turned folk song genres, particularly the ballad, into high-culture poetry in the years from about 1800 to the 1930s, from Wordsworth through late Yeats. The German *volk* needed an English counterpart; in 1846, William Thoms, an amateur antiquarian, suggested the old word "folk" and the new coinage "folklore." It's a suitably vague word that took the place of terms like "popular antiquities." Thoms's words made "folk song" and "folk music" possible, as well as the founding of scholarly institutions, such as the American Folklore Society in 1888. Amateurs like Thoms gave way to professionally trained academics in the emerging English, anthropology, and music departments of expanding universities, the ancestors of today's ethnomusicologists.

The *Oxford English Dictionary* lays out a wonderfully diverse set of meanings for the word "folk," which goes back centuries. Since that English word swept the world as part of an American wave of musical influence, it is worth thinking about its range of reference.

Sometimes it just means "people" in general, while other early citations suggest subordination to God or the higher classes of society. But it can also go down home, as "the people of one's family," or even connote the individual, as opposed to the group. Attached to "song," folk can either refer to "a song originating from the common people" or "a modern imitation" of that type of song.

Some of these contradictions and layers of meaning, which still influence folk music, started when certain eighteenth-century Enlightenment thinkers argued for a tolerant universalism that favored local culture. In 1773, the literary critic and philosopher Johann Gottfried Herder (1744–1803) said that every *volk* had its own forms of expression, especially including folk songs. He approved of being broad-minded about the varieties of human experience, but this type of tolerance often took a back seat to growing pseudo-scientific theories that graded the human species into unequal races, with white Europeans on top. And it even came up against the steady rise of nationalists. They saw local folklore as a core of nation-state bonding in a highly competitive struggle for power and resources. It was an age of continental wars, revolutions, and colonial expansion. Herder extolled the particularity of German national identity, and indeed, Hegel's word *Volksgeist* (1801), the "spirit of the folk," could serve as a sign of people's everyday cohesion or as a rallying-cry for passionate patriotism.

The intelligentsia quickly realized that folk music could help shape society in their own image. Smaller nations, often subordinated to stronger states, leveraged their identity through folklore, including music, dress, vernacular architecture, holidays, food, and, above all, language. The Finns, caught between the powerful Swedes and Russians, were among the first to center their sense of nationhood on oral traditions. By 1835, one intellectual, Elias Lönnrot, cobbled together surviving scraps of Finnish epic tales to create the national saga, *Kalevala*. By then, upper-class activists had also composed their own "folk songs" in artful arrangements that trickled down to the folk themselves. Collecting and disseminating folk music has always been a two-way street, featuring back-and-forth, up-and-down circulation between an urbanized intelligentsia and the rural masses who make up the majority population.

At the same time, dominant societies repressed local styles. As mentioned earlier about the "keening" tradition, in Ireland and Wales the authorities banned folk musics and musicians. Queen Elizabeth I even ordered the elimination of Irish harpists in her 1603 order: "hang the harpers, wherever found and destroy their instruments." Across Europe, local conditions and attitudes varied. In Hungary around 1900, the great composer Béla Bartók's work of collecting and promoting folk song seemed radical. There, the musical taste of the still-prestigious nobility tended toward sentimental urban melodies worked up by professional Roma musicians. The songs of the unwashed, untrained peasants ranked low until Bartók's international compositional success opened people's eyes and ears.

In the United States, folk music definition split along the racial lines of the 1800s. For Americans, indigenous peoples took the place of European "primitive," their "savagery" eventually tinged with sentimentality as the tribes were pacified and thus "doomed to vanish." The quest for Native American folklore became one of the main goals for the new American Folklore Society, defined as collecting "the fast-vanishing remains of folklore in America," with a tilt toward American Indian material. The very first doctoral dissertation in musicology written by an American on *any* music research topic was penned by Theodore Baker in 1882 and titled "On the Music of the North American Savages." Baker had to go to the University of Leipzig in Germany to do his degree work.

Meanwhile, African American music, originally part of the experience of slavery, remained in a "peculiar" position. It could not exactly be "folk music," which belonged to the rural white majority. Cecil Sharp, the great English folk music activist, came to Appalachia in 1912. He was hoping to find preserved remnants of old English folk song. He did a great job of collecting the melodies of the mountains at a time when Americans were just beginning to take them seriously. But he scrupulously ignored any ties to the black musics also indigenous to the region. He said that the white highlanders had "one and all entered at birth into the full enjoyment of their racial heritage," creating a "community in which singing was as common and almost as universal a practice as speaking." Yet in Sharp's day, it was on urban stages that the average American consumed a large amount of so-called black folk music, as parodied and re-created by white performers in blackface

Cecil Sharp

Cecil Sharp instigated the "first English folk revival" in the early years of the twentieth century in several ways: intensive collecting in rural England, the publication of a seminal study (*English Folk Song: Some Conclusions*, 1907), the propagation of songbooks for schools and the public, the revitalization of Morris dancing, and the founding of the English Folk Song Society (1911). Sharp's work persuaded the composer Ralph Vaughan Williams, among others, to use folk song in his concert works.

Sharp made a pilgrimage to the United States in 1912–14 to follow the trail of English folk song to Appalachia, building on the budding collecting he found there. He produced a groundbreaking two-volume work, *English Folk-Songs from the Southern Appalachians* (1932), that viewed the American southeastern mountaineers as an untouched sanctuary of "organic" living and singing. A leftist critique of Sharp as a bourgeois, prudish nationalist took hold in the 1970s, changing academic opinion about this foundational figure whose work nevertheless remains a cornerstone of folk song research in both Britain and the United States.

in the most popular form of the nineteenth century, the "minstrel show," and offshoots of those productions, such as the medicine show, reached more isolated places reasonably quickly.

Eventually, with a broader sense of national identity and the success of the recording industry, African American music came to be appreciated as a source of, and eventually as an influence on, mainstream American music. Yet the focus on British Isles origins—and later on black music—meant that it took until late in the twentieth century for Latino, Jewish, and many other ethnic groups to be recognized for their roots folk music. Striking miners in Appalachia in the twentieth century might have been listening to a Hungarian band as well as an English tune, but that

The Seeger Family

Charles Seeger was an original and sometimes thorny thinker whose writing and activism encompassed musicology, ethnomusicology, composition, and music theory. He worked on folk music collecting, administration, and publishing in a number of federal agencies from 1936 to 1953. His second wife, Ruth Crawford Seeger, a noted modernist composer, contributed folk-song studies. Of Charles's children, Pete has had the greatest public influence as singer, songwriter, and activist. A key figure in the "folk revival" that stretched from the 1940s to the early 1960s, he was a member of the Almanac Singers and the Weavers. Pete Seeger suffered anticommunist blacklisting in the 1950s and beyond, but eventually became a much-honored living legend and a mentor of Bruce Springsteen. Mike Seeger played a pivotal role in promoting little-known American folk musicians and as part of the New Lost City Ramblers; Bob Dylan has called him "the supreme archetype" of a folk musician. Peggy Seeger has carried on similarly influential work after moving to Great Britain, originally teaming up with her husband, Ewan MacColl, to spur the folk revival there.

possibility does not figure in the national imaginary about the coalfields. Other regional styles were overlooked. Writing about the upper Midwest group The Goose Island Ramblers, all of northern and central European heritage, Jim Leary says that "the neglect of upper Midwesterners generally requires nothing less than a reassessment of what constitutes American folk music."

In other regions around the world, the story played out under conditions set by Europeans. For hundreds of years, travelers, missionaries, and colonialists heard folk music around the world. They often disdained local folk songs but paid tribute to what they thought of as ancient, "civilized" high-culture music, concentrating on the courtly traditions of the kingdoms of the Middle East, India, and China. Jaap Kunst, a Dutch scholar-administrator living in Indonesia, who coined the word "ethnomusicology" around 1950, made a specific instrument-set, the gleaming bronze *gamelan* of the Javanese sultans, famous, rather than the songs of villagers. He was responding to the standard three-part model of the world's musics: *oriental* to describe the ancient-civilization approach, *primitive* for all the indigenous musics of Africa, Oceania, and the Americas, and *folk* for the "internal primitives" of Europe: the peasants and farmers.

Globally, this set of divisions of the world of music spread, as local intelligentsia members adopted or adapted the Euro-American idea of intellectual intervention. In Latin America and the Caribbean, the Europeanized upper class downplayed the traditions of indigenous peoples and the imported African workforce in favor of a search for "Hispanic" styles as the basis for national music cultures. In the "oriental" zone, local elites also neglected folk music in favor of what the West had defined as being of value: court and urban professional styles and histories. In parts of Africa, the influence of missionaries downgraded or suppressed village musics, as also happened in Oceania. As these regions emerged from the long cultural shadow of European domination, they began to rethink vernacular music. Martin Stokes says, for example, that "folk music is presented

Béla Bartók and Zoltán Kodály

Béla Bartók, sometimes working with his fellow-composer Zoltán Kodály, pioneered vast, fundamental folk-song fieldwork in Hungarian, Slovak, Romanian, Serbian, and even Turkish and Arabic territories, beginning around 1900. This brought regional and world attention to Central European and Balkan folk musics. As a scholar, he developed super-precise transcription and analysis procedures that created a benchmark. As a composer, he transformed his findings into a distinctive and influential personal style that did not imitate folk music, but rather infused concert music with the insights of folk composers about rhythm, melody, and articulation of musical thoughts. Bartók kept a professional and class distance from the folk musicians he recorded, but he deeply respected their creativity and appreciated them as compositional colleagues.

The longer-lived Kodály heavily influenced Hungarian music as a socialist bureaucrat, and he gained fame with a system of elementary, folk-based music pedagogy, still used in many countries today.

by many musicians and folklorists in Turkey as a timeless and self-evident fact of Turkish cultural life," and "is considered by its proponents and practitioners to play a specific role in creating a culturally unified and cohesive nation-state."

Folk music meets the bureaucrats

From the start, governments had a strong stake in folk music. The regulation of working instrumentalists goes back to medieval and Renaissance times in Europe, as a way for city fathers to control celebrations and the activities of a potentially dangerous class of citizens. Still, in remote parts of Norway, "plenty of fiddling went on that was not for pay, and thus was not subject to regulation . . . certain venues were difficult or impossible to keep under official control," such as "the regional markets" where "fiddlers met and exchanged tunes."

The growth of the nation-state only intensified the urge to regulate folk music, coupled with the need to support local traditions. In other words, the official managers of music have tried both carrots and sticks to this end. From promoting internal cohesion through stimulating exportable culture, planners and promoters have worked from the top down to create bottom-up change, circulation, and control. Whether for monarchist, socialist, or democratic agendas, bureaucrats have taken charge of what is supported, allowed, and sent abroad. Eventually, mainly in the United States, academic patrons and gatekeepers took on some of these functions, in the name of education and enlightenment. But first came the state, as early as the late 1800s, across Europe, from Britain to the Balkans, channeling official energy through school systems, songbooks, and sponsored singing societies.

The most flamboyant, and maybe the most studied, chapter of this history unfolded under socialism, from 1917 to 1991 in the Soviet Union, and from around 1949 to 1989 in central and southeastern Europe, and still today, to some extent, in China, Vietnam, Cuba, and North Korea. Bureaucrats located folk music at the intense intersection of ideology and nationalism. What better way to justify Bulgarian or Romanian state control than to see it as the will of a singing and strumming "people" of single purpose and identity? Donna Buchanan summarizes the situation in Bulgaria as she unpacks the official term *narodno*, based on a Slavic root that can translate into English as both "national" and "folk": "Because it collapses the folk or traditional, ethnic, national, and people's into a single construct, *narodno* lent a sense of historicity and hence legitimacy to post-1944 socialist customs, whether we consider the bestowal of the federal award title *Naroden Artist* (People's Artist) or the significance of *narodni ensemble* (folk ensembles)." The chain of command that linked villages to the capital cities in these societies was so intricately braided that no simple flowchart can describe its strands adequately. Talented village musicians were brought to town to undergo professional formation, which reshaped their sense of self. They "became travelers, physically and intellectually, circulating fluidly amongst hamlets, municipalities and transcontinental megalopolises" as the government built folk music into an export industry.

This chapter in the story of folk music began first in the Soviet Union, where the creative and managerial genius of Igor Moiseyev sketched the blueprint for the "folk song and dance ensemble." Starting in the dark days of the Stalinist purges in 1937, professional performers "perfected" dance steps and strumming patterns of the countryside. The argument ran this way: the noble folk, essence of our *narod*, is too busy working to develop a polished act, but the state provides the possibilities of doing just that: isn't it a fitting homage to their labor, and isn't it beautiful? Moiseyev, who died at the age of 101 in 2007, defined his own handiwork as "a spiritual portrait of the nation." Seventy years after the ensemble's first performance, the *New York Times* offered this assessment of the group on tour: "the dancers bring a convincing humanity to what they do, despite the company's resemblance to a well-oiled machine. Their smiles seemed unforced, and they watched and responded to one another in performing that looked freshly minted."

Moiseyev's approach spread worldwide over time, from China to Africa. The Soviet model spread to socialist-minded states in early postcolonial Africa. In countries such as Guinea, Ghana, and Senegal, governments assembled village performers into subsidized troupes, systematically making a dance and music melting pot that blended local styles into a national brand, which could help both to unify fledgling states and create a platform for global identity. A troupe

Web site in Ghana still states this: "If there is any one artistic group that has given credence to the claim that our culture is exportable, it is the National Dance Company of Ghana (Ghana Dance Ensemble)." This group is part of the National Theatre, which describes itself as "professionally equipped to meet world standards with unique and viable customer-oriented programming in the contemporary and traditional Arts. At the National Theatre, it is world class all the way," unconsciously echoing the phrasing of the old Soviet approach.

Within the core socialist states, internal diversity presented problems as well as potential. In Bulgaria and Romania, Romani ("Gypsy") musicians provided much of the pizzazz of local music-making through their appearances at weddings and festivities. But official ideology made it impossible to define this marginal ethnic group as shapers of what was *narodno*. So they simply ceased to exist and were folded into mainstream culture. No scholars could study or publish Romani repertoire or identify their contribution. The regimes imposed the same ethnic erasure on all ethnic minorities in both countries: Jews and Muslims, Germans, Hungarians, and Turks.

But in the vast multicultural space of the Soviet Union, the cultural commissars had no choice but to let Uzbeks be Uzbeks. The many republics and "autonomous regions" produced their own folk systems, as long as, to use Stalin's phrase, the resulting music and ensembles were "national in form" only, but "socialist in content," whatever that meant to censors and purges at the moment. One of the most intriguing inventions of the bureaucratic brain emerged with the rebuilding or "perfecting" of local musical instruments. For all of Central Asia, a "laboratory" in Tashkent undertook to remake lutes, fiddles, and flutes. This meant modifying the local scale systems to suit the standard modern European tuning found on the piano, away from microtonal modalism. Frets were added to fingerboards to ensure conformity. The builders dreamed up families of instruments of different sizes, on the model of the violin-viola-cello-bass quartet of the symphony orchestra. Spectacularly synchronized sounds based on chords and arrangements replaced the solo and small-group traditions of the old folk musics of the region.

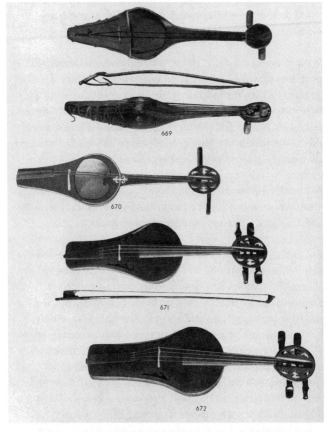

5. Traditional and modernized forms of the Kyrgyz *kyak* fiddle showing the rebuild from the older solo, horse-hair, gut-laced version to the new family of violin-viola-cello-looking instruments built for orchestral sound.

On a visit to Central Asia in 1968, my jaw dropped upon hearing the overture to *Carmen* played on these newfangled instruments, and I naively asked why this needed to happen. The designers looked surprised: why should Central Asian musicians stay stuck in obsolete traditions when they could be up to "the level of world culture?" They reassured me that local artists could still play the old music if they wanted to, but I wondered how they could, since the esternized frets glued into their factory-made instruments made the old scales impossible to produce.

State management operates in many places and many levels. Since 1981, the government of the Indian state of Tamil Nadu, home to 62 million people, has certified a handful of folk musicians, "making sure the folk artists are okay and making sure that the village arts are developing properly," in the words of one bureaucrat. These lucky performers receive liberal support and many opportunities to perform, but only after proper preparation. As the official says, "we can help the groups with training, costume design, staging, and presentation." Other, noncertified musicians can only look on enviously as they scuffle for work. Moiseyev is alive and well in twenty-first century South India.

The liberal democracies in the wealthy countries also like to steer folk music's change—ever so gently—from offices far removed from the action. In the United States, the Smithsonian Institution has run the National Folklife Festival since 1967. Each year, more than one million visitors brave the broiling heat of Washington, D.C., to roam through tents and exhibits set up at the very heart of American culture, the Mall. With the Washington Monument looming as a backdrop, American states and invited national delegations represent themselves in precisely programmed ways. Why? In 1989, the head Smithsonian bureaucrat saw the event "celebrating freedom" and said that "citizens of our nation and the world must be free to converse with one another." A few pages down, the festival's organizer, Richard Kurin, said "we do the Festival so that people can be heard . . . to help legitimate alternative forms of aesthetics and culture... [that] meet Smithsonian standards of authenticity, cultural significance, excellence." But also "so that practitioners may be encouraged to pass on their knowledge" and, ultimately, to "symbolize aspects of our own nation and sense of community." That is a serious set of aims and goals. Some observers have leveled the criticism that organizing creative folk artists in this way restricts rather than empowers them. But Kurin also points to the innovation that the festival encourages, as it "generates its own traditions" and "new culture is created" by throwing together people of very different backgrounds and places. The government claims to ensure that folk music both endures and expands its options.

This cultural activism could come about only when the United States changed its mainstream ideology from one that assumed or enforced "Anglo-conformity," or waited for a new culture to emerge from "the melting pot" to the new ideal of a consensus that stressed "multiculturalism" and "diversity." This shift synchronized with the change of immigration laws in 1965, which radically altered the demographics of the United States, bringing in newcomers from Asia and Africa with new cultural configurations. The National Folklife Festival is just one manifestation of the local, state, regional, and national urge to "celebrate" a sometimes standardized set of group identities. Canada entrenched this idea with a federal Multiculturalism Act in 1988, but this only created, rather than subdued, a debate over top-down musical management. Early on, presentation was "too often token and decorative," and some regions felt underrepresented, while Aboriginal nations thought the new lingo just marginalized them more.

Europe too has seen shifting attitudes toward folk music. Once thought of as the essence of a unified people and the bedrock of national identity, folklore's position has changed dramatically in the past couple of decades as the presence of permanent immigrant communities has reshaped the cultural landscape. What if some people's customs and folk songs get on other people's nerves or simply sound too "foreign" to keep up the fiction of a single national expressive culture?

One study in Denmark showed that teenagers were very eager to consume outside musics of the transnational world-music type, but were not in the least inclined to listen to the music of their foreign-born classmates (e.g., Kurds)—they were just too close, yet still too alien, for comfort. City- and state-supported efforts to get minorities to represent themselves publicly bump up hard against mainstream indifference but also the internal maneuvering of minorities, who might be subdivided into very different groupings of language, politics, and musical aesthetics.

If societies run into unexpected upheavals, old-fashioned folk music nationalism can reshape musical forms more ominously. Around the same time that the Danish students were being polled, the country called Yugoslavia disappeared from the world map, fracturing into new states that had gone to war with each other. Musics that were enjoyed multiculturally suddenly separated into ethnic emblems. Serbs, Croats, and Bosnian Muslims played the *gusle*, a one-stringed fiddle of the storytelling singers who captivated male coffeehouse crowds for days on end, singing epic tales of olden times. Suddenly, when the Serbs began the siege of Sarajevo, they amplified the sound of a *gusle* player even as they attacked and killed hundreds of civilians, a version of sonic terrorism that changed the face of folk music. Meanwhile, in the Croat capital of Zagreb, the *gusle*-playing folk musician Mile Krajina claimed a different identity for the very similar tradition of tale-telling by appearing in 1990 with the nationalist party leadership to celebrate Croatia's new nation-state status. The *gusle* is just the public face of a huge redefinition of local, regional, and ethnic folk styles in the region by nationalist media, governments, and political parties.

Less politically motivated, but no less agenda-driven, colleges and music schools began to dynamically direct folk music toward broader audiences, beginning in the 1950s. The United States pioneered in casting folk music into the academic mold of its expanding higher-education system, beginning with the Institute of Ethnomusicology at the University of California at Los Angeles and the World Music Program at Wesleyan University in Connecticut. Academic training has given the seal of approval to collecting and teaching practices that earn university jobs and college credit. Initial excitement eventually turned to careful consideration and even soul-searching among academics. They constantly reconsider the liberalizing rhetoric about the musical enlightenment students achieve by playing in a Javanese gamelan, a Mexican mariachi group, an African drumming class, an Andean panpipe ensemble, or a Trinidadian steel band. Elsewhere, institutions from Holland to Australia have linked up in a worldwide organization called Cultural Diversity in Music Education (CDIME), which meets in a different country every two years to discuss issues such as the theme for the 2010 conference in Australia, "The Cultural Aesthetics of Teaching," a far cry from the work and attitudes of early folk song collectors. Interactivity with local populations and reconsideration of older values marks today's intellectual intervention.

Chapter 4
Collecting and circulating

Folk music meets the machine

When Thomas Edison had his assistant recite a nursery rhyme
into a primitive recording device in 1878, he had no idea that the
little machine would change the fate of folk music forever. By
1890, the scholar Walter Fewkes tried out the new equipment on
the Passamaquoddy Indians of Maine, taking the first documented
collecting trip. It was just a warm-up for his more extensive work
among the Zuñi people in the American Southwest. Soon enough,
professional and amateur folklorists and anthropologists were
visiting many tribes, farms, and villages, not just in the United
States and England but all over the world.

The folk themselves had mixed reactions to this mechanical
incursion. Some saw it as a magical form of robbery or a breach
of custom. Even in the United States, the response could be
violent, as Erika Brady reports: "the venerable Omaha singer
Utah Atoning, who died shortly after recording with Francis
La Fleche in 1916, was said to have been killed in retribution
for having divulged sacred material." Other American Indians
seized the chance to preserve their language and songs, turning
the tables on white attempts to wipe out indigenous cultural
resources.

6. The earliest form of collecting: a young man transcribing his grandfather's memoirs by hand in Brailov, Ukraine.

Folk Music

The relations between the folk and the collectors could be dynamic. The pioneering English folk song collector and activist Cecil Sharp credited his recordings of a Gypsy woman with saving his life, when he played them for her jealous and threatening husband. Aside from possible fears about the intimacy of the recording session, Sharp generally had little use for sound recording. He thought singers produced stiff, rehearsed versions when they sat down in front of the machine, and much preferred to write down their spontaneous performances by ear.

How to behave when requesting—or demanding—a recording session became a hot topic among the intelligentsia. The bossiest approach came from the tireless, prolific ethnomusicologist Frances Densmore (1867–1957), who offered some details of her working practice to a budding collector asking for advice. She was very blunt about who was in charge: "The singer must never be allowed to think that he is in charge of the work. A strict hold must be kept on them."

68

7. Classic European folksong collecting: Zalman Kiselhof recording folksongs onto an early wax cylinder device around 1912 in the An-ski Jewish folklore expedition to the southern Russian Empire.

Densmore exerted maximum control to make sure that no second of the precious, limited recording space on her discs would be wasted, so advised that "all yells must be strictly forbidden...it is also a waste of space on the blank to let them 'talk' and announce the song in the native language, etc." She completely controlled the performance, refusing to allow singers to use their folk instruments: "an Indian drum does not record well, and a rattle does not record at all." She even did a personality search: "singers should be checked by general reputation." She was staying true to the basic philosophy of the early twentieth century of all types of collections, in museums, public exhibitions, educational settings, and archives: get a standardized sample that is as "clean" as possible for easy understanding and quick comparison across a huge range of objects. Songs were just another specimen to be collected, catalogued, and analyzed. Today, we regret Densmore's erasure of her singers' natural voices, asides, and announcements, all of it valuable and unrecoverable cultural information about folk music.

Over time, folk music collectors grew ever more sensitive and sophisticated in the ways that they gathered, interpreted, and analyzed what they heard among unfamiliar populations. Densmore's impulses of control gave way to subtler ways of interacting with singers. Tony Seeger, a longtime collaborator with the Suya, an Amazonian rain forest Brazilian people, discovered that "the mutual effort to understand each other was often tiring and frustrating for everyone involved . . . they had their own busy and complex lives to lead, and some of my questions were unthinkable, others were unanswerable, if they could be understood at all." So he had to blend in better: learn more of the almost unknown Suya language, so that "my questions became more interesting to them." He learned to drop back into the setting, intervening less and observing more, since "the Suya were not required to have us at all." Eventually, he found ways to bridge the gap by long-term, repeated visits that gained trust and by helping the Suya with their relations to mainstream Brazilian culture, including making recordings to spread understanding.

Ultimately, Seeger decided that "the most rewarding public projects for ethnomusicologists will often come from the desires of the community members themselves" and became "convinced of the importance of using the results of our research in places far beyond university walls for the benefit of the communities whose music we study." Under the banner of "advocacy" and "applied ethnomusicology," these recent principles have radically changed intelligentsia–folk musician relationships. But even the best relationships produced thorny questions. David McAllester, who worked with Navajo ritualists for decades, got agreement from the healer Frank Mitchell and his family to film a restricted ceremony, the Blessingway, only by promising that no one could view the movie unless McAllester was in the room. But as he grew older, the ethnomusicologist wondered what to do with the footage: assign someone else the viewing rights? Give it to an institution—but who could he trust? Simply leave the film on top of a sacred mountain to melt into nature? Ultimately, he passed the viewing rights on to his daughter and his archive (now located at Wesleyan University), which only delays the ethical issue he raised.

The ambivalence of collectors appears in the pioneering work of figures such as Laura Boulton, who called her memoirs *The Music Hunter* and who supported that image with pictures of herself in a pith helmet, commanding chiefs to sing for her. Even the great Béla Bartók, while championing the everyday songs of the Hungarians and creating a personal compositional style inspired by the folk, did not actually want to live with or spend much time with the peasants he admired as fellow-composers. Early ethnomusicologists dipped in and out of the lives of folk musicians, as compared to the more conscious collaborations of recent decades, which have led to long debate and publication about the potential and problems of "applied ethnomusicology" and "advocacy."

From North America to Australia, what to do about all that early recording has raised serious questions of cultural equity for some years. "Repatriation" means giving people back the artifacts and even the bones of their ancestors, but it took a long time for that term to enter the conversation about musical ownership. When the work finally started in the 1980s, it became clear that it is actually easier to give back their musical heritage to groups than it is to return other types of memory traces, since an archive can make identical copies both for itself and the descendants of the musicians. Still, as Charlotte Frisbie says, "groups have different attitudes about what should and should not come home, and, if so, when, where, and how it should be handled, what should then be done with it, by whom, and for what purposes."

It is no wonder that groups such as the First Nations of British Columbia in Canada need to carefully consider how to deal with repatriated materials. As early as 1884, the government outlawed their ceremonial practices of conspicuous gift-giving ("potlatches") on the basis that they were "incompatible with Western economic practices and inimical to the concept of private property." Many musical instruments and other artworks were smashed or confiscated. With the potlatch law repealed only in 1951, it has taken a long time for these peoples to develop and create their own museums and living heritage programs for the returned objects.

Today's new flexibility toward storage and give-back of group memory allows for creative, interactive forms of folk music collaborations. Here is how an Australian archive of Aboriginal folklore describes itself: "The Mukurtu Wumpurrarni-kari Archive is a 'safe keeping place.'...Mukurtu is the Warumungu word for 'dilly bag.' Warumungu elders used to keep sacred items in dilly bags to ensure that they were kept safe. The archive uses the cultural protocols of the Warumungu people to arrange, sort, and present content. Any piece of content that is not marked 'open' (and thus viewable by the general public) is tagged with a set of restrictions." This innovative approach allows individuals and families to keep their own archives private, yet available to be shared "in-house," while allowing broad access to everyone in the Internet community for approved materials. And the group gets to organize the presentation.

This new Internet-based accessibility might help Australians over the barriers that Alan Marett describes, and could lead people to the appreciation he wants to emerge from the research that he hopes he has done well: "Knowing that some songs are 'secret' and potentially harmful [if heard by the wrong listeners], people...choose to avoid them completely. This has inhibited the degree to which Australians have been able to engage with Aboriginal music, and this in turn has affected the extent to which Aboriginal song is known and appreciated both within Australia and internationally." He feels that, under proper conditions of respect and control, "most Aboriginal communities, at least in the north of Australia, want their music to be more widely disseminated and better understood.... I tell you, it is worth engaging with these songs. I only hope that I have done them justice."

As researchers fanned out across the globe in search of songs to study, they crossed paths with commercial collectors looking for sources of income, not knowledge. In 1909, the Gramophone Company of London sent a collector more than two thousand kilometers (1,249 miles) across the Caucasus and Central Asia to find music fodder for the markets of the Russian Empire. The corporation had being doing business in the region since 1901, and by the time of the Revolution in 1917, it had produced four thousand recordings. Meanwhile, in New York City, the growing record companies did not need to hire caravans but simply to commute from New Jersey to the teeming immigrant communities, with their many musicians. The Victor Company's E-series produced nearly six thousand ethnic records by 1920. The American companies pushed their dealers to reap the profits from their investment, as a 1914 in-house bulletin for record sellers announces: "Getting the foreign trade is not a mysterious art or science...the 35,000,000 foreigners making their home here are keenly on the alert for anything and everything which will keep alive the memories of their fatherland...if you are not getting your share of it, you are overlooking a large and profitable business which, moreover, is right at your door."

Victor's rhetoric is far more pro-immigrant than the politics of the time might suggest, coming as it did just as "antiforeigner" sentiment was moving toward the closing of mass migration to the United States in the early 1920s. The profitability of this market declined sharply with the rise of radio. Companies moved away from the East Coast to the rural and southern interior, allowing the folk music of those regions—including both white and black forms, religious songs, blues, and dance tunes—to be

Collecting and circulating

73

commercialized only two decades after big-city ethnic groups, from Albanians to Norwegians, had had their turn.

All this activity gave shrewd ethnic musicians a chance to maximize their opportunities. The Jewish bandleader Abe Schwartz not only recorded for Columbia under his own name but also was the person paid (but not listed) for Polish and Russian bands (Orkiestra Wiejska and Russky Narodny Orkestr), which boasted the same Jewish American musicians. Like other immigrants from Europe, Schwartz was able to turn his natural folk versatility in playing for many clients' weddings into the new studio situation, which favored fast turnover and quick labeling. Folk thinking means that the information on early record labels is far from reliable. Someone like the clarinetist Dave Tarras, who recorded as both a Jewish and a Greek bandleader, would spontaneously give a track a title he thought might make commercial sense, rather than help future researchers looking for authenticity.

These many-sided musicians, like their colleagues worldwide, had to deal with the seismic shift in musical playing and listening habits that early recording unleashed on folk music. The dizzying 78 rpm of the fragile discs limited performances to 2½–4½ minutes. Across the world, singers and musicians who were used to unfolding their musical thoughts in a leisurely fashion had to condense and cut. Initially, sound quality favored strong-profile instruments over modest ones—clarinet trumped flute, piano eliminated zither. The resulting tracks were lopsided, too; sometimes it's hard to tell just what the lineup is on a given track. Almost mysteriously, the old engineers put in more material than they could extract on the primitive playback devices of the day, such as wind-up Victrolas. Today, digital sound reconstruction can dive into those grooves and come up with the pearls of sound that the recording encased but which the older technologies could not deliver.

Like the sound in the grooves, most folk music recording got covered over as time went on. With the arrival of radio in the

1920s, the worldwide depression of the 1930s, and the end of mass immigration in the United States, people stopped buying specialized, relatively expensive records. But the 1940s saw folk melodies resurfacing on record in America. Little labels looking for specialized markets discovered all kinds of subcultural sounds, including African American styles not in the mainstream, children's discs, and eventually what we would call world music today. Folkways Records, started and run by Moses Asch for decades, became the home of people such as Woody Guthrie, Pete Seeger, and even the very young Bob Dylan, making it possible for newer generations to pick up on music from the margins. At the same time, Asch literally left his door open to researchers returning from Albania, the Congo, or Burma. By keeping every record continually in print and accumulating a list of some two thousand albums, Folkways left a legacy of folk music that continues to influence the repertoire, especially after the Smithsonian Institution took over the label in 1987. Still keeping the old discs in print, Folkways also produces new top-quality folk music albums every year and makes a great deal of its music available online.

With the invention in the early 1950s of what we now call "vinyl," the 33 rpm record with at least twenty minutes per side, folk music possibilities opened up considerably. Little labels like Folkways got competitors, most notably from the Nonesuch Records series, that could present longer performances and better sound quality. By the 1980s and the rise of the CD format, the restless industry giants decided to make their move and coined the term "world music," which had circulated on campuses at the first ethnomusicology programs, such as those at UCLA and Wesleyan University. This looks like a rerun of what the Gramophone Company had done eighty years earlier, but now with jet travel and digital recording, as well as better advertising, a small but effective market emerged that has supported the emergence of world-class stars, largely from developing countries. Instead of selling world music to immigrant and local ethnic communities, the cartel aimed at new audiences of dance-floor enthusiasts looking for pulsating beats.

African musicians supplied the main muscle of this marketing. Many of them from francophone countries flocked to studios in Paris. Treated as outsiders, these musicians were expected to stay with homegrown sounds, but they had larger ambitions and wanted to expand their range. Conflicts emerged between the patrons and the artists over "modernization." Performers claimed the right to move from the margins to the mainstream in arrangement and song writing but risked losing their valued exoticism. At the same time, producers felt free to arrange folk songs from previously obscure corners of the world, often without asking permission or offering payment to the folk musicians themselves. Steven Feld traced a song of the Ba-benzele Pygmy singers of the African rain forest as it blended into arrangements by a number of first-world artists, and followed the song of a small band of Polynesian islanders as it moved into a successful world-music album, and then as the basis for the jazz stylings of the Norwegian saxophonist Jan Garbarek.

This free-market approach to musical materials took center stage with Paul Simon's top-selling album *Graceland* in 1986, which relied on South African inspiration and back-up musicians. Some saw it as opportunistic co-optation, while others pointed to the subsequent success of the group he hired, Ladysmith Black Mambazo, as a kind of compensation. Was it collaboration or exploitation? What has been clear from the beginning of commercial recording of folk music remains true: many musicians get underpaid and slip into obscurity, while others reap the rewards of the system. The payoff can be dreadfully delayed, as in the situation of Solomon Linda, who in the 1930s wrote what became the song "Wimoweh," an all-time folk song hit, mutated by the magic of Pete Seeger into a campfire classic. Decades after his death, the royalty arrangement with Linda's family has only recently been arranged after many false starts.

Zora Neale Hurston and John Wesley Work III

The African American author Zora Neale Hurston studied anthropology at Columbia University under the pioneer scholar and highly influential teacher Franz Boas, who encouraged her to undertake fieldwork in the American South. Hurston incorporated folklore materials in both her fiction (*Their Eyes Were Watching God*, 1937) and nonfiction writings (*Mules and Men*, 1935; *Dust Tracks on the Road*, 1942).

John Wesley Work III, collector, folklorist, and composer whose work was based in African American folk music, collaborated with Alan Lomax on Mississippi fieldtrips in 1941 and 1942. Recent writings assert that Lomax did not give Work and other African American colleagues from Fisk University enough credit for their contribution to his research and writing.

Songs in circulation

Both researchers and record companies have deeply influenced the circulation of folk music, both within and outside the source communities. In the nineteenth century in the West, songs moved in and out of print. Collectors and schools put out songbooks that had their own impact on collective knowledge and memory. Sound recording added an extra channel to this flow, and people could hear their own songs from new media. Some of the "old" tunes gathered by state-sponsored fieldwork might just have been a folksinger's version of a recording. Starting in the 1920s, radio made its own contribution to this mix. Live performances of "old-time" music moved straight into rural and urban living rooms, with all the power and immediacy an up-to-date technology could offer. When people see and hear the media valuing their music, it can give them a new sense of value for old songs and tunes. It can also influence the way they sing and play their instruments.

Conversely, commercial folk music recordings have had a massive impact on the recent musical developments and figures, from popular to classical. Perhaps the most striking example is the rural blues, and most emphatically those recorded by Robert Johnson (1911–38), a short-lived, obscure musician who has attracted more attention and reverence than any other folksinger in history. He has been the subject of countless writings and has even appeared on a recent U.S. postage stamp. Johnson's handful of 78 rpm recordings inspired Bob Dylan to say: "Whenever I [listened to him] it felt like a ghost had come into the room, a fearsome apparition...Johnson's words made my nerves quiver like piano wires." After the initial shock, Johnson's posthumous presence liberated Dylan's creativity: "If I hadn't heard the Robert Johnson record when I did, there probably would have been hundreds of lines of mine that would have been shut down—that I wouldn't have felt free enough or upraised enough to write."

Complex flows rippled out as these early African American commercial guitar-based discs flowed to musicians like Dylan. Davy Graham heard them in England and crafted a personal instrumental technique in songs such as "Angi," which then cycled back to the United States for a young New Yorker named Paul Simon to discover as he modified "roots music" for his own neo-folk guitar style. For years, countercultural Moscow bluesmen sang in synthetic southern American accents, fomenting fandom with words they couldn't understand.

All this slow percolation of tunes, performance styles, and attitudes has dramatically accelerated in the twenty-first century with the coming of the Internet. The first place to turn for any kind of folk music is YouTube, which came into existence in 2005. What used to take hours or months to track down now takes a few seconds. Unreliable as the sources may be, unstable in terms of production values, and impermanently housed as they are, the endless samples of the world's folk music available online through this and many other sites (some listed at the end of this book) have blurred the line between commercial and collector mentalities, retail, and research, in ways that will only multiply in the future, with uncertain implications for the history of folk music.

One way to sort out the multiple possibilities of musical flow is to sketch the biographies of the songs themselves, rather than institutional or personal histories. At any moment, you can take a snapshot, a day in the life of a song, and see, as in a family album, growth and change, shifts in styles and personnel, even as the resemblances keep striking the eye and ear.

Take the song "Old Paint," for example. During the 1910s to 1940s, a formative period for what would become the "heritage" of American tunes, this waltz-time "farewell" tune circulated in and out of print and recordings, from a Wyoming saloon to the New York ballet stage in that brief but intense period. In 1908, the pioneering folklorist John Lomax went down to his native Texas on a college scholarship from Harvard University, encouraged by his ballad-studying professors to look for authentic American folk songs. The incongruity of a Texan needing to be sent off from Harvard was not lost on Lomax, who writes about the disbelief of the cowboys he met, who could not believe that collecting their songs made any sense at all. He ran into a college friend—more Harvard here—in a saloon in Cheyenne, Wyoming, and after they sang college songs, his buddy Boothe Merrill gave him "Goodbye, Old Paint," describing it as the last waltz at a cowboy breakdown, or party. Sure enough, Lomax heard it at "a rollicking play-party" in Texas. The play-party was a type of entertainment run by religious-minded parents who held that fiddle tunes were sinful, but that singing and clapping the same tunes was okay for carefully monitored teenagers to dance to.

In 1927 Carl Sandburg, a famous populist American poet, published a very influential folk song collection, *The American Songbag*. He

John and Alan Lomax

In 1910, John Lomax wrote the trailblazing *Songs of the Cowboys,* based on his Texas roots and fieldwork. Supported by government-funded cultural projects in the 1930s, Lomax, assisted by his son Alan, created a canonical archive of American folk song and singers, including Woody Guthrie and Huddie Ledbetter ("Leadbelly"), future anchors of the 1950s "folk revival," and Muddy Waters, who eventually became a rhythm and blues star. Both John and Alan Lomax are sometimes critiqued for manipulative or condescending attitudes toward their collaborators. Alan heavily influenced world folk-music diffusion and reception as a popularizer (tour manager, radio and television host, songbook compiler, author), tireless collector of traditional repertoires in both the United States and Europe, and analyst. He devised universalist theories of folk music based on statistical studies, or "cantometrics," as well as "choreometrics" for folk dance. His original albums, a landmark series, have been reissued digitally with updated notes.

called it "a ragbag of strips, stripes, and streaks of color from nearly all ends of the earth," recognizing America's diverse population. He included "I Ride an Old Paint," which he got from Margaret Larkin of Las Vegas, New Mexico, who heard it from a buckaroo "last heard of as heading for the Border," and said, "the song smells of saddle leather." With most of the *American Songbag* songs, Sandburg turned to professional musicians to provide piano accompaniments. He would sing the tune for the composer, and they would work together on a mutually acceptable arrangement. As to why he needed to varnish the plain wood of the songs he valued so highly, Sandburg said: "there is an added lighting or tincture given them." But there is an intriguing agenda in Sandburg's strategy, found in this telling sentence: "This is precisely the sort of material out of

which there may come the great native American grand opera."
Behind the populist mask lies the high-culture planner.

If not a grand opera, perhaps a ballet: in 1942 Aaron Copland, the
composer who most clearly defined a lasting American style in
concert composition, received "Old Paint" from the choreographer
Agnes DeMille as part of a set of tunes for *Rodeo*, a sequel to
Copland's successful folk-inspired score for the ballet *Billy the Kid*.
A part of Sandburg's dream of moving his song collection onto
the concert stage was realized by a leftist, gay, Jewish New York
composer whose mother, though born in Russia, had grown up in
Illinois and Texas and whose grandfather was a peddler who traded
with American Indians. Perhaps having read John Lomax's origin
story for the song, Copland set it as a plaintive waltz at a cowboy
dance, preserving something of the original context along with his
orchestral variations that poignantly picked the tune apart into
wistful melodic musings.

Even as Copland was elegizing the frontier for the concert-hall crowd,
John Lomax was memorializing "Old Paint" in his way by recording
for the Library of Congress in 1942 versions of the song from two
Texas cowboys, Jess Morris and Sloan Matthews. Morris gave such
a personal and detailed account of the song's origins that it has
eclipsed Sandburg's origin story and even Lomax's own memory of
meeting his Harvard buddy in Wyoming. Morris says that when he
was seven years old, in 1885, he learned the song from Charley Willis,
his father's black hired hand, which gives "Old Paint" an African
American grounding. The true story of the black cowboy has only
recently emerged from the all-white image of the classic Hollywood
Western. Given the long life of "Old Paint" in American collective
memory, Charley Willis deserves a starring role in this new scene.

Jess Morris's version of the song carries its own historic weight,
since his performance style and even the words he sings are
distinctive and unique. He starts with a personalized fiddle
introduction, and punctuates the tune with the sound of the

violin, not an instrument that the average American associates with cowboys. The 1930s invention of the "singing cowboy" on stage and screen, starting with Gene Autry, put "cowboy" and "guitar" together permanently in memory. Morris uses his own fiddle tuning to create a modal, moody sound that both contrasts and blends with his emphatic punching out of the song's syllables in the strained, tense timbre that the folklorist-musician John Cohen would later call "the high lonesome sound." By contrast, the other 1942 archival recording, by Sloan Matthews, falls into a comfortable, lilting time with only some overlap in the lyrics, showing both how widespread and how locally variable a single song could still be in mid-twentieth-century Texas.

Meanwhile, in 1941 and 1944, the legendary folksinger Woody Guthrie recorded "Old Paint" twice, offering more snapshots for the song's family album. Guthrie learned the song not from his ramblings and wanderings across America but from Alan Lomax, who provided Woody with the Larkin version that ended up in Sandburg's *American Songbag*. This would seem to be an

Ex. 7. **"Old Paint" as sung by Sloan Matthews for John Lomax, 1942. Transcribed by Mark Slobin from Rounder CD 1512, *Cowboy Songs, Ballads, and Cattle Calls from Texas***

My foot in the stir-rup, my po-ny won't stand, ____ Good-bye Old Paint, I'm a-lea-ving Chey-enne

intellectual intervention into Guthrie's vernacular world of the American Southwest, but, typically, Woody played around with the song, re-folklorizing it by adding a verse (not on the recording) praising his "dark skin woman" this way: "Her breast is sweetest that I ever did press / And her skin is the warmest that I ever felt." Much more in the vein of the working-class poetics he is known for, Guthrie added this verse for recording: "I've worked in your town, I've worked on your farm / And all that I got is this muscle on my arm."

From its heyday in the 1940s, "Old Paint" did not fade away. To the contrary; it had probably its highest moment of visibility in 1952, in the classic Western *Shane*, where it is banged out on a piano at an outdoor cowboy dance. Though the film stays true to the older evidence that the song was used as the last dance, the couples do not do the waltz, instead trying out a more stiff and stately step. The orchestrated version that Hollywood created bears a strong resemblance to the Copland setting, probably not a coincidence. "Old Paint" refuses to disappear, circulating in various formats down to today. Two top-selling and influential artists put out their versions between *Shane* and now: Johnny Cash in 1965 and Linda Ronstadt in 1978. Cash was following his own interests in the American West when he recorded *Johnny Cash*

Ex. 8. "Old Paint" as sung by Jess Morris for John Lomax, 1942. Transcribed by Mark Slobin from Rounder CD 1512, *Cowboy Songs, Ballads, and Cattle Calls from Texas*

Fare-well, fair lad-ies, I'm a-leav-in' Chey-enne, Good-bye, my lit-tle Do-ny, my Do-ny won't stand.

Sings Ballads of the True West. He read John Lomax and Carl
Sandburg on the subject, so it is not surprising that his version
reflects those sources, continuing the chain of influences. In his
liner notes, Cash claims authenticity: "How did I get ready for
this album? ... I slept under mesquite bushes and in gullies ... sat
for hours beneath a manzanita bush in an ancient Indian burial
ground, breathed the West wind and heard the tales it tells only to
those who listen." But he also defends updating the old songs: "We
aren't sorry for the modern sounds and modern arrangements
on classics like "I Ride an Old Paint" or "The Streets of Laredo";
after all, they were meant to be heard on twentieth-century record
players and transistor radios!" The album was not a big seller.
The 1960s was apparently the wrong moment for a cowboy song
compilation, though Cash's performance lives on, in Internet
format.

Linda Ronstadt's album *Simple Dreams* is one of the twists and
turns she made through multiple stages at the peak of a very
successful career that led her from rock 'n' roll and "folk-rock"
to country and pop. She presents "Old Paint" as a medium-slow
waltz with slide-guitar shadings and wistful vocals. Ronstadt
keeps inspiring a number of women to post themselves online
singing "Old Paint." One, who bills herself "Faceless in Seattle,"
keeps her head down under a large cowboy hat as she strums;
another says that singing this kind of song helps her when she
comes home from a difficult job. But trolling the site also turns up
an aging band called "The Arthritis Brothers," and a very young
Chinese American boy at an electric keyboard, with everyone
finding something in "Old Paint" that drives them to appear in
public as performers. This type of ongoing folklorization draws
on the many printed and recorded versions that have piled up
over the decades. In a very democratic way, it continues the
process of personalization that is so essential to the idea of folk
music, whether carried on by the lone cowboy like Jess Morris
improvising in the sagebrush, individualist recording artists such
as Cash and Ronstadt moving through phases and genres across

a long career, or little Brandon Ho at his keyboard in his living room, posted, probably by admiring parents, to the Internet.

There are many twists and turns on the road that folk music travels, often built by outsiders, not the folk themselves. Take the case of the union members who didn't really pick up on the songs that Pete Seeger and his friends tried to stir them up with in the 1930s and 1940s. The repertoire really clicked a little later, among well-educated city people. The working folk select their favorite sound-patterns as part of an ongoing strategic and creative effort, which gets them through their challenging and often perilous lives. It is a strategy for survival. Even under the most horrifying conditions, such as the Nazi-rigged ghettos of the Holocaust, Jews sang their favorite songs, often changing the words to fit their endangered existence. Everyday invention remains a powerful force, even in the most dire and dangerous landscapes that folk music can inhabit.

Beyond the continuous invention that still keeps folk sources flowing in many social settings, the music feels the effects of techno-management and formal frameworks. Some of this activity bubbles up from inside small musical worlds and across modest networks, while much of it flows into the lives of artists and communities in waves of energy from the outside, in top-down fashion.

Chapter 5
Internal upsurge: movements and stars

Folk music's long evolution—from countryside comfort and celebration to urban and mediated music-making—wells up from internal needs and desires as much as from external pressures and possibilities. For instance, the first fiddling contest in Norway—back in 1881—was started by fiddlers, not the government, which then tried to co-opt the energy. Regional pride and ethnic identity run deep everywhere. Satisfied societies sing, but so do stressed-out ones. The many actors in the drama of folk music quietly or dramatically play out their resources, strategies, and agendas. Every stage-managed festival and marketed recording shares time with live musical action in town squares, union halls, churches, temples, and taverns.

The momentum of movements

Individuals project their voices—literally and figuratively—through their music, and their efforts can parallel, jumpstart, or coordinate with the needs of collectives, sometimes organized into social movements. The mill girls who left their country homes to work in America's first factories sang handmade songs to pass the endless hours of work, to cheer their limited leisure time, and to lament their lot. Folk song as a form of resistance goes back to earliest recorded times, dating to the age of peasant uprisings, and flourished among people forced into new work conditions. Eric

Foner, chronicling labor songs, says that already by 1836, a former farm girl in Massachusetts could create a new kind of folk song, homemade but in an idiom designed to be sung at a strike:

> Oh isn't it a pity that such a pretty girl as I
> Should be sent to the factory to pine away and die?
> Oh! I cannot be a slave / I will not be a slave.
> For I'm so fond of liberty / That I cannot be a slave.

Though this young woman could deploy the word "slave" metaphorically, it had a far more literal meaning for the Africans forcibly brought to the Americas. In the 1840s, slaves composed new folk songs in extreme conditions, as William Wells Brown reported: "The following song I have often heard the slaves sing when about to be carried to the far south: 'See these poor souls from Africa / Transported to America / We are stolen and sold to Georgia / Will you go along with me?'" The fairly formal diction of this song contrasts with the terse testimony of another slave song of the period (converted here to standard English from the dialect spelling of the day): "We raise the wheat / They give us the corn / We bake the bread / They give us the crust / We peel the meat / They give us the skin / And that's the way / They takes us in."

Music channels strong sentiments, thus circulating into many kinds of movements, conservative and progressive, religious and radical, or even a combination of more than one motivation. Homesickness and protest, lovesickness and religious fervor can flow through the repertoire of a single singer or community at a particular moment, without contradiction. Those activist New England mill girls also sang comically and sadly about love, as did the slaves.

But it is the steady stream of songs of protest that have lingered longest, still being sung in many places and situations wherever people gather to complain and demand. Those songs rose to the surface in the very active social turbulence of the 1930s to the 1950s. Pete Seeger, who knows a thing or two about social-movement songs, nicely catches the overlap between the personal and the collective: "like hymns and patriotic songs, union songs are songs with a message…unlike most hymns and patriotic songs, union songs are usually composed by amateurs to suit a particular occasion, and have a short life. More often than not, they are simply new words to an older melody."

This quote goes to the heart of folk-music practice in modern times. Occasions produce lyrics, which often have a message about conditions of life. Working people frequently come up with these texts themselves, stimulated by shocking events such as the collapse of a coal mine, the crash of a locomotive, or the falling of a tree, anything that suddenly wipes out everyday people. The words appear in newspapers or circulate by word of mouth and enter the folk song system, very often without an author's name attached. Even if the original creator gets credit, variation quickly emerges, rephrasing the words to suit local events and personalities. Sometimes an organized social movement—say a labor union—puts together a songbook that recirculates the songs, like the well-known songbook of the International Workers of the World, aka the Wobblies, in the early twentieth century. Recordings amplify these efforts and allow the songs to go great distances, sometimes around the world. Increasingly effective personal technologies facilitate the musical domestication that brings folk songs into new homes, linking listeners in ever-widening ways.

Social movements don't have to be "progressive" to flourish musically. Many thousands of people over many years can organize their music and advocacy around an energizing one-word, value-laden cultural concept. "Celtic" is a fine example. The historical Celts burst onto the historical stage more than two thousand years ago, expanding across much of Europe and dealing major blows to the Roman Empire. They seem to have always been fond of music. Their speech evolved into languages spoken today in parts of Ireland, Scotland, Wales, Brittany, and the Isle of Man.

But the imaginary Celts occupy a much larger territory in the mind of millions of people who enjoy and reshape music they think comes from an ancient heritage. "Celtitude," with its ever-changing content and forms of music-making, keeps thriving and evolving for all kinds of reasons. Yet as Lois Kuter points out, "no one has identified specific structural, melodic, or rhythmic elements that can be isolated as Celtic." Fairly recently, the Galicia and Asturias regions of Spain have joined the Celtic music movement, based more on a sense of historic and folkloric ties than a clear linguistic connection to the other Celtic zones.

In the twentieth century, "Celtic music" offered a fine example of internal upsurge, a kind of pushback against the domination of the British and French (and possibly Spanish) nation-states that tried to suppress alternate forms of political and cultural expression. The number of people who could speak Celtic languages kept dwindling, so much local energy was channeled into the music, more easily kept alive outside the oppressive institutions of the school and the government. By the mid-twentieth century, the various streams of Celtic music-making became tributaries to a broader river of events, recordings, and touring bands that united previously separated traditions in the region. As Martin Stokes puts it, referring to the Irish, Breton, and Welsh festivals, "Where language often divides (but shouldn't), musicians, many of whom are experienced hands in the cross-cultural and multilingual worlds of the *fleadh*, the *fest-noz*, and the *eisteddfod*, are often the only people able to shape a shared aesthetic space."

Celtic music is a multi-carat musical diamond of many facets. Illuminated by research, activism, and marketing for decades, it simultaneously sparkles in the eyes of individuals seeking self-fulfillment, local performing groups, far-flung Internet communities, seasoned festival managers, and transnational traders of down-home sounds. Desi Wilkinson, an Irish flute player closely connected with traditional Irish dance music, says that in Brittany, a local festival called the *fest noz* "has become vitally important as the symbolic focus of a whole range of activities...an inclusive celebration in which everyone participates, from the singer, musician, or dancer to the server or client at the bar." The modern *fest noz* of this sort developed only in the 1960s, decades after Irish musicians turned musical house parties and pub nights into national competitions, or the Scots converted fiddle and piping contests into showcases for national identity. Once established, this festival system seeks partners, and not always just in the Celtic world. Deborah Kapchan relates why Breton musicians might want to go on tour with Moroccan colleagues: "By performing with the Gnawa on the festival circuit in Brittany, they are telling a story to themselves and others, a story about their victimization and their cultural perseverance." The festival organizers say that Celtitude can be roughly equated with the African "Negritude" movement for cultural autonomy, despite what she calls a "troubling" lack of overlap.

Each Celtic region has its own history of the ups and downs of folk music enthusiasm, but all move in the direction of greater social organization. In Wales, the downturn in traditional styles caused by industrialization and religious repression was itself reversed from the 1930s on by amateur societies, which began to both revive and regulate public performance. These efforts held the fort for folklore until the recent linguistic revival and loosening of central British authority was able to lead to more systematic educational and media efforts aimed at solidly grounding local identity.

Calling all this activity "Celtic" throws a nebulous cloud over much regional activity and seems fatefully tied to modern media. At the extreme, Wilkinson continues, "Celtic music is not shared, but it is exchanged. Its space is not personal and acoustic but public and mediated. Celtic music only exists after it is produced and marketed; it has no existence outside its commodity form." To what extent does all this musical mediation count as "folk music?"

As always, that depends on the definer. From the marketing point of view, small-scale sales, often local, consign artists to the "folk" margins of merchandising. Players and listeners may also decide that they need the term to distinguish their tastes and performances from the "pop" world. As with the term itself, folkness is up for grabs at any point in the chain, from practicing to recording to festivalizing to consuming and cherishing.

A trip to Australia both localizes and complicates the picture. There, in the 1970s, Graeme Smith says, Celtic music helped to define the creative tension between different social layers: the descendants of the original Anglo settlers, the post–World War II migrants from various places, and the beleaguered Aboriginals. It all culminated in "the 1970s folk-rock bush band musical style, which embedded Irish traditional dance music into musical narratives of Australian national identity and the use of the [Aboriginal] *didjeridu* in Irish music." Smith sees this as a hopeful turn of events: "the musical blending of Aboriginal and Irish musical traditions holds the promise of new grounds for racial and political reconciliation, as well as … a history in which both the premodern Irish and the contemporary Aborigines participate in a generic tribalism." Meanwhile, back in Ireland, the same *didjeridu* is associated with Celtic Bronze Age horns that "directly address a collective and ethnic subconscious."

Stokes goes so far as to compare Celticism with the transnational power of contemporary pilgrimage, as he speaks of "a globalized resurgence of a Celticism expressed in a religious idiom." Indeed, some internal upsurge in folk music arises from a genuinely religious impulse, for example in Bosnia. As described by Mirjana Lausević, the story of the emergence of the *ilahiya*, a sacred song, begins in 1990, just before the collapse of the country called Yugoslavia, of which Bosnia was a subdivision. The Bosnian Muslims are Slavs, who adopted Islam over the five hundred years of Turkish rule in the region. They sang hymns—*ilahiya*—not so much as a form of worship but as a folk tradition, with mothers crooning them to babies to pass on the ideals of Islam. Texts in Arabic or Turkish were transformed into Serbo-Croatian (now Bosnian), the local Slavic language. In the socialist state of Yugoslavia, this kind of dedication to religion was discouraged, so the *ilahiya* circulated quietly as a kind of folk song. But in 1990, cracks in the official culture of the country grew, and a Muslim party won local elections. A tape of *ilahiya*, sung by Muslim high schoolers, circulated widely and even became commercially successful. This wave of interest crested in a huge event at a soccer stadium for believers, featuring *ilahiyas* arranged for the stage, with polished and more complex musical arrangements. These new songs had Arabic and Turkish texts, moving the hymn away from a local vernacular sound to a more international Islamic orientation that helped encourage strong feelings of national identity among Bosnian Muslims. As one audience member said, "everyone breathed with one soul and one song" at the concert.

The horrifying war that followed shortly after the concert only helped to cement Bosnian Muslim identity, which now holds steady in a situation of continued tension in the nation-state called Bosnia, patched together from warring populations and managed by the international community. The *ilahiya*, which helped to sustain the beleaguered Muslims during the war, continues as cultural grounding, once again sung in Bosnian. This folk song genre functions at a high level of professionalism, pointing in three directions: (1) inside, to offer stability after destruction and dislocation, (2) outside, to the Islamic world as an emblem of locally colored affiliation, and (3) worldwide, to the Western music scene, with an eye to the world-music market.

Celticism and the Bosnian *ilahiya* are just two examples of conservatively oriented internal upsurge, as opposed to the more familiar progressive ring that folk music tends to have in general. Though extremely disparate, all of these examples of grassroots activism rely on a stable sense of folk music as an organic, elemental, and defining agent in personal, community, national, and even transnational life. These urges can help to unify small, scattered nations such as those on the Solomon Islands, in Melanesia. The 'Are'are musicians of Malaita were cited earlier for their subtlety as theorists of their folk music. But that internalized system has recently expanded outward, as part of a more global consciousness. Today, young Solomon Islanders have worked up older ensembles to project the sense of a united culture. Their concert program cites "political divisiveness and instability" and affirms that "the traditional performing arts, particularly panpipe ensembles, serve as a common element that bridge the nation's diverse islands." Youth bands use their hard-won music income from a tour to Hawaii to fund a local health clinic—grassroots folk music can indeed be literally constructive.

From country to city

This organic notion of folk music runs into deep trouble when rural people leave settled spaces and move to cities, for reasons of displacement or opportunity. Dislocation decenters, but it also opens up opportunities for new expressions of affiliation. We have some fine descriptions of this process of rethinking roots music. Most celebrated, perhaps, is the great black migration in the United States from the South to the North, which brought the fabled bluesmen to Kansas City and Chicago. But less well-known migrations have reshaped the destiny of folk music worldwide, in waves that began as early as the eighteenth century in England and continue to this day in the megalopolises of Asia, Africa, and the Americas. We looked earlier at the collective music of African mining migrants; in Brazil, the move from 75 percent rural to 75 percent urban happened just between 1940 and 2000; worldwide, in the early 2000s, a majority of human beings found themselves living in cities for the first time in the species' history. The following four examples of emerging urban musics tell very different tales about how people create new folk music with the materials they bring to cities.

Thomas Turino has given a fine, focused account of what happened to the music of highlanders from the Peruvian Andes, who moved to the capital, Lima. This large-scale migration created a flow and counterflow, as people and media moved new music from the city back to the mountains. By the 1980s, it was no longer possible for Turino to do old-fashioned fieldwork in the small upland communities, since "much of what influences rural indigenous musicians and musical style is ultimately traceable—through medium-sized highland cities—to Lima itself as the hub of the national society." Meanwhile, in the capital, music became "a safe cultural marker for the migrants," as opposed to the more obvious signs of identity that mainstream Peruvian society might censure: "language, consumption of coca, and the *t'inka* ritual of offerings to divinities of Aymara-speaking regions." By concentrating on the seemingly innocuous woodwind sound of the *sikuri*, the highland panpipe, migrants found "the path of least resistance in relation to the dominant group's aesthetic dispositions while still being a distinguishing emblem."

Typically for this kind of internal upsurge, the urban folk music strategy boils down to creating official organizations that can set standards for musical performance, and organize venues and contexts for public presentation. This kind of planned structure can then serve both purposes: internal identity and external acceptance. As an activist originally from the highland town of Puno told Turino, "We Puneños, through the regional clubs, have begun to change the culture in Lima.... It used to be that we *provincianos* and our culture were not accepted in Lima, but now there are even *sikuri* ensembles performing in the *center of Lima, in the streets!*" The situation Turino describes in Peru maps the flow of a single immigrant stream to a metropolitan center. In many other places, urban immigrants come from many different backgrounds, opening up the possibility of multiple styles intertwining to create new, shared musical fabrics. The model of indigenous panpipes in the streets can then freely flow to the streets and subways of major cities worldwide.

Christopher Waterman's classic study of Lagos, Nigeria, maps a dazzling array of newcomers and their musical tastes. Together, this multifaceted population built a layered city culture. It anchored the well-known Afropop styles that energized the world-music scene of the late 1980s. One driver for this exciting musical transformation was the open-minded aesthetic of the dominant group, the Yoruba. By the 1960s, they had invented "hundreds of named musical genres." Significantly, "music appears to have played some role in the construction of social networks among African workers in Lagos," so it had more than just entertainment value.

Not all of these new urbanites simply came from up-country villages, as in Peru. Two important musical influences flowed in from repatriated Africans—former slaves who returned to Lagos. The Aguda had lived in Brazil and Cuba, so brought a whole array of music, from Catholic chants to varieties of carnival music such as *samba*, which joined the African mainstream. The other returnees had been freed by the British even before they left Africa, and so returned from neighboring countries to Nigeria, bringing all manner of styles from the coastal regions. Rootsy and personal, their "palmwine" songs arose from the fact of being crowded together in challenging city circumstances but in a local society that enjoyed the expressive payoff of creative combination.

A similar story in eastern Europe took a completely opposite turn. As described by Ljerka Vidić Rasmussen, the huge influx of villagers to big cities in former Yugoslavia started off by collaborating to make lively mixed music. The country was a socialist state with a difference: the government allowed a modest commercial recording industry to spring up. In more than one city, then, city composers and singers could combine Serbian and Macedonian rhythms—one symmetrical, the other asymmetrical— with Bosnia's florid singing style and by slowly standardizing instrumental arrangements to make an attractive folk-based style with cross-ethnic appeal. This music was dubbed "Newly Composed Folk Music" (NCFM), a seeming contradiction that only underscores how flexible and powerful roots musics can be, and it became the country's best-selling style, despite the import of Euro-American rock and other competing genres.

But as the country began to disintegrate, regional consumers began to pick apart the coalition. The more western-European-oriented zones of Slovenia and Croatia looked outward, and the Serbs looked inward to their eastern Slavic heritage. This left the Bosnian-Macedonian sound, still very popular, sticking out as something "oriental" to audiences thinking past a nationally unified music, and a dispute arose about the sound's credibility. During the war, each country emerging from the ruins of Yugoslavia rethought the materials of the folk sources, as suggested earlier about the differential use of the formerly shared *gusle* fiddle (see page 65). Re-tuning the components of more urbanized NCFM, post-Yugoslavs shaped a blatantly nationalist, sometimes militaristic music (Serbian "turbo-folk") or, as in the Bosnian case just mentioned, rejected secular sounds for the sacred song the *ilahiya*. Urban immigrants turned into redesigned, militant citizens, literally marching to different drummers. Even folk roots can be radicalized under the pressures of violence and dislocation.

South Africa, no stranger to these pernicious processes, tells still another story about urbanization. As Carol Muller explains, three kinds of city immigrant stories have emerged from long-term processes of worker influx, each with its own destiny. *Maskanda* (the word comes from the Afrikaans *musikant*, or musician) arose from what Zulu men heard while working on the farms and in the houses of white owners, who sang their own European songs. Like the American slaves of the nineteenth century who modified their masters' music into songs or dances (such as the cakewalk), these sharp-eared Zulu listeners domesticated European songs, even adapting them on Western instruments such as the concertina and the guitar. A second stream of music coming out of urban migration, "gumboot," fuses sources as disparate as German missionary tunes, Russian folk dances from sailors, and American tap and jazz styles, which urban immigrants turned into an energetic, complex set of styles for communal celebration. Muller says it "is neither essentially African nor Western, neither Christian nor ancestral, neither traditional nor modern. Much like its migrant practitioners, who are neither fully urban nor fully rural, gumboot dance has long existed in the interstices of South African society."

The third style of the emerging South African cityscape, *isicathamiya,* is the best known, because of its association with musical globalization, ranging from Pete Seeger's folkie, campfire song "Wimoweh" in the 1950s to Paul Simon's highly commercial 1980s *Graceland* recording project. The point is that each of these three South African styles has emerged from intricate multi-ethnic, global interaction patterns, while still maintaining the folk roots that make it valuable to the displaced villagers who continue to cherish and develop it over the decades.

And each genre gets progressively standardized. For gumboot, it is communal consensus about how celebrations should be organized, and for *isicathamiya* it is the intersection of the community and the music market. *Maskanda*, on the other hand, the least visible of the three, formalized in academia, when the University of Natal started a festival in 1993 to "rejuvenate passion" and increase visibility for this neglected genre. This idea worked: *maskanda* began to appear in the media and to circulate abroad. This had the effect so common to evolving roots musics: strong performers seize the opportunity to develop personal styles, the level of performance rises as a result of emerging stars and continuing contests, the music finds new venues and contexts, and moves out, seeking commercial support. Thus, migrants to cities take their wandering ways into the world, usually with very mixed and sometimes surprising results for the original communities and their musical sensibilities.

Personal pathways

Across the world, energetic folk musicians have an inner drive to carry their childhood music across boundaries. Some barriers are social, some geographic, others economic. Starting with their innate ability to communicate through sounds, these pathbreakers universalize local experience, creating new resonance and echoes wherever they go. In each case, different doors have opened to allow such musical travelers to pass through, or they have pushed them aside themselves. The second half of the twentieth century broke open old closed systems. It was a turbulent time of change, ranging from the end of colonialism in Africa and Asia, the beginning of minority recognition in the West, and the reshaping of the world-music market through globalization.

Among the earliest to take advantage of such opportunities was Babatunde Olatunji (1927–2003), whose eloquent autobiography narrates his personal pathway and philosophy. Born in a Nigerian village, Olatunji felt the urge to move on: "you know, the world is bigger than the village. Today, I see my mission as global." He became one of those migrants to Lagos mentioned earlier. He appreciated the variety of styles the big city offered, and seized the chance to study in the United States in 1950, following his cosmopolitan instincts. Living first in the pre-integrated South and then in Harlem, this dynamic drummer responded to a rising interest in things African, both among African Americans and a larger subset of Americans looking for new sounds and pastimes. As Olatunji realized, "the spirit of the drum lies in knowing how to play what can be evocative, what is powerful enough to make people stop and listen, to make people feel something that they cannot find the words to describe, but that they can experience." Though written about how he understood the power of village music making, the quotation applies equally to his both heartfelt and canny sense of how to appeal to multiple audiences in very different social settings. "This era was so full of excitement and challenges to everybody who was alive and part of it, black or white." Olatunji mixed with civil rights leaders, jazz greats, and presidents, blazing his own trail against a backdrop of discrimination, social change, and the simultaneous deep appreciation of what he could offer. By 1958, he had a breakthrough show in New York that led to major television appearances, and he began to dream of establishing an African music center and a network of schools that would spread the music and the message that began with rural folk music.

As the century and Olatunji aged, the emerging world-music scene provided him with ever-expanding networks of performance and activism. Mickey Hart, once the drummer of the Grateful Dead, created the "Planet Drum" project that combined Olatunji with other folk-oriented drummers. New Age and other self-fulfillment movements wove various strands of music and philosophy into performative practices that spread across the United States and the Western world. Olatunji made "very sure that my presentations at those places are geared toward the message of togetherness and love, and that everyone is allowed to feel important." Here the personal side of folk music's evolution operates at two levels: the star on his cosmopolitan quest to spread his music and philosophy, and the seeker of inner transformation. Olatunji noticed the particular appeal of his message for American women: "In Santa Cruz, out of a class of 200, 150 may be women." Drumming, always a male drive in his home village, turned out to have implicit power that could change Western women's sense of self.

Along the way Olatunji had to tack with the winds, adjusting his sails to the situation. The American factory-built drums, though supposedly ecologically safe, posed a challenge to the African master. As Eric Charry points out, he must have had "mixed feelings" about these synthetic instruments, given that "his philosophy of the healing power of drums was based on the trinity of spirits inherent in the tree and the animal skin that make up the drum and the human player who brings it to life." Stars shine, but their light bounces off an earthly social surface.

The career and life of Yuri Yunakov (b. 1958), a Bulgarian-born world-music star, tell a tale that has more contrasts than similarities with that of Olatunji. While the African drummer was marked for local chieftainship in his Nigerian village, the Balkan saxophonist has struggled since childhood with a question mark over his identity. Carol Silverman, who has both studied and sung with Yunakov, says "he could never be fully accepted by Bulgarians, because he is Muslim, Turkish-speaking, and Romani." He suffered considerable abuse in Bulgaria, to the extent of seeking, and gaining, asylum in the United States, where he settled among Macedonian Roma (Gypsies) in New York, who see him as a Bulgarian.

In New York, Yunakov quickly adapted, becoming fluent in Albanian, Armenian, and Middle Eastern styles in order to serve local audiences and gain a reputation. Internationally, he is an "exotic," with a successful career: "European audiences perceive Roma as an imagined last bastion of tradition in a modern Europe devoid of authenticity." This attitude provokes a creative crisis for many "roots" musicians who want to expand the range of their expressive palette. Yunakov, like the Senegalese superstar Youssou N'Dour, has trouble with managers and listeners who insist that he not use the synthesizer instead of "folk" instruments. Just as he resisted the Bulgarian socialist regime by going beyond the narrow musical niche carved by bureaucrats, so he continues to push back against outsiders' definition of his musicianship.

Still, Silverman continues, Yunakov remains "not only a versatile musician but also a practical strategist. He is a consummate collaborator and, unlike most Balkan musicians, initiates diverse musical contacts for possible future business." Where does this leave "folk music" in the constellation that this star inhabits? It depends on the angle of vision. Close-up, in a city like New York, communities of Balkan and Middle Eastern immigrants carry on older folkways that depend on bands for celebration, as they do back home. Indeed, musicians circulate between the United

States and Europe regularly to keep both sides happy. Families send wedding videos across the Atlantic, all of which feature a strong musical profile. This opens up another view, a panorama of resettled but restless folk who want to be multi-sited in their families and tastes. Zooming farther out, the scene reveals a transnational picture. It strongly favors attractive folk sounds, along with the allure of colorful characters, which consumers identify as coming from a different space-time continuum than the everyday world of the Western metropolis.

But as enjoyable as it is to consume folk music, the feeling can only go so far. Some people get so drawn in to the experience that they get the urge to jump in themselves. Across the developed world, from Sydney to Tokyo to Stockholm, individuals put their ears, muscles, and heart into making music that is, in some sense, folk. The shy woman who signs herself "Faceless in Seattle" appeared earlier in the discussion of "Old Paint." Alone in her room, cowboy hat on, she relives the Old West's folklore. Her decision to mount a Web-cam to capture her efforts makes her performance part of collective consciousness. Her quiet video lies at the far end of a spectrum, with the other end located by the deafening drumming of a *taiko* group at an outdoor festival in Santa Cruz or Rotterdam. At home, online, or in a crowd, personal participation shares a single drive—the musical attraction that draws people to an instrument or style the way iron filings fly and cling to a magnet.

No easy formula can explain why sometimes even large numbers of people will find such satisfaction in what they call folk music, as happened in the 1950s folk revival in the United States. This movement rapidly and successfully spread to Europe and remains as a cultural touchstone in many formats ever since. Was it the "alienation" of post–World War II youth, turning away from materialism, in combination with parallel social emergences, such as the hippie and beatnik sensibilities, as some commentators pronounce? But the movement was too multifaceted to sweep under one analytical rug. Campus coffeehouses for black-clad folkies or hip hootenanny hangouts had little in common with the mainstream television versions, featuring the top-selling, clean-cut Kingston Trio–type bands, or the bongo drums and berets of Hollywood teen flicks. None of that activity needs to be lumped together with the power of "We Shall Overcome" and the other political-action songs and singers of the civil rights movement, although overlaps can be found in common family trees, particularly that of the Seegers.

Today's affinity groups keep only the dimmest echoes of that bygone age of revivalism. Two very different folk music–inspired scenes will stand in for hundreds in the following discussion. Together, they create a sweeping set of circles, formations of devoted individuals who come together in person or on the Internet to pledge allegiance to a cherished music under the banner of folk.

Mirjana Lausević, who came to the United States as a graduate student from Sarajevo, found herself popular among Balkan music and dance groups as a "native" who could teach. She thought at first that these Americans must be of Balkan descent, and was amazed when she realized they were outsiders who had freely chosen to deeply invest themselves in all things Balkan, from performance, clothing, décor, and food to pilgrimages to southeastern Europe.

Her book, *Balkan Fascination*, digs deep into American history to explain that such patterns go back to the nineteenth century, for all sorts of reasons, ranging from physical education courses at Wellesley College to settlement-house programs in city slums to folk revival–era activists. Today's Balkanites, who tend to be white, well-educated, and middle class, do not feel themselves to be "ethnic." They are simply drawn by the magnetism of a moment of contact, often vividly describing first-time experiences that alerted them to the music and dance. For example: "I looked into this room and people were folk dancing. I did not even know what it was but just thought it was the neatest thing. So, I just became completely obsessed with it. I mean, I danced every night." Or: "I remember the first time I went folk dancing. It was a magical moment."

From these formative flashes of attraction, Balkanites often move on to workshops and summer camp gatherings, which offer them a sense of community. They feel these sites embody the original spirit of the folk world: "This camp was so special to me because it was the closest thing ... to the real Balkan experience, real village experience." They might well suffer "post-camp withdrawal" as they return home and come down from the peak experiences they have just had in the pastoral, idealized setting of the camp-village. Many Balkanites even create ensembles, and Lausević found that at least 60 percent of her informants had traveled to the Balkans, sometimes for long stretches of time.

As to why these eager adepts feel the pull, many say that they are looking for deeper meaning in their lives: "I think the American culture is very hollow and we wanted to fill it with richness that we saw in other places." This sentiment echoes throughout the world of Western affinity groups, whatever the point of origin of the folk spirit that people find so fulfilling. A foreign music seems like a cozy cabin in the wilderness of contemporary culture. In describing how the music works its magic, Balkanites can be either very specific—"it's because of drone. Drone roots it to the earth"—or quite general—"it spoke to me, it felt ancient to me, it felt natural to me."

These descriptions build on very old foundations of antimodernist sentiment, the very feelings and drives that led to the identification, collection, and propagation of folk music two hundred years ago and more. They also coincide with the most recent craving for premodern lifestyles and activism around organic foods, sustainable economies, environmental awareness, and self-fulfillment through "healthy" products and practices. Lausević remarks that "consumerism and a museum mentality are definitely evident in the Balkan music and dance scene." Seeing the Balkans—or any preindustrial region—as home to all that is good and natural is a leap of the imagination, given the real state of things, and can easily arise from misunderstandings or wishful thinking. As mentioned, Roma musicians valued for their musical skills suffer indignities and armed attacks regularly in eastern Europe, which is why artists such as Yuri Yunakov do not necessarily view their homelands in a rosy light. Organized groups and sensitive scholars of the music and dance try to bridge the gap between the imagined and actual life of southeastern European societies to allow Balkanites to continue to enjoy and evolve their affinity-group folkways.

So many types of affinity groups abound that it is hard to survey this huge field of contemporary folk music activity. Sometimes just a musical instrument, by itself, can stimulate a vast field of practice, like the *djembe* drum that has engendered a thousand drumming circles. One especially vivid example of a wildfire from a small spark is the *didjeridu*. This is essentially just a hollow log, quietly and deeply developed by groups of Australian Aboriginal peoples for internal ritual practices. Peter Hadley has studied the immense dispersion of this instrument that, "especially since the 1990s, has gone from being an esoteric oddity to the focal point of Internet communities, Web sites, and gatherings and festivals around the world." The instrument or, more precisely, the idea of the instrument—a long sounding-tube—has moved geographically, physically, and conceptually far, far away from its place of origin among non-Aboriginal people, raising issues Hadley points to: authenticity (is there a "real" didjeridu and are others "fake?"), control (is the instrument "somebody's," so that others have no right to it?), personal and community identity, and the whole range of possible permutations of both the object and its meaning. Complicating the whole situation is the lack of Aboriginal initiative in promoting or shaping the didjeridu's global destiny, even though there are some well-known players of Aboriginal origin. The spread of a worldwide network for this instrument begins in a folk setting, among peoples once isolated, then overwhelmed and suppressed by an incoming European wave. Turned into myth, the Aboriginals' cultural essence distills into a single object, made from a log. Its very simplicity makes the "didge," as it is nicknamed, into a template for creative rethinking, rebuilding, and networking.

Worldwide, musicians may either try to identify with the Aboriginal folk origin or to distance themselves from it. Some actually meet with native practitioners and collaborate with them; some simply read up on the subject. In Hadley's interviews, the word "respect" kept cropping up as a marker of recognition that the music one is drawn to and loves "belongs" to someone else, a feeling much more prominent in the didjeridu world than among Balkanites. Just as many strategies of empathy and identification can appear, even more ways of distancing can evolve. None arise from lack of consideration for the instrument's origins; on the contrary, respect can drive a musician to distinguish his or her own work with the didjeridu from how it all began, to make a statement of separation as a gesture of understanding difference. Simple tinkering with the object itself, making it from different materials or souping it up electronically, has built new branches onto the log, turning it into a global tree of resonance. Then, composers can set to work placing that sound in as many different contexts as possible, from pop music to chamber music to New Age meditative albums, universalizing a sound-ideal. A network of Web sites, festivals, and recordings allows personal improvisation and craftsmanship to become a musical movement that is, in its own way, a folk music world.

A new mythology has indeed sprung up, grounded in the "organically spiritual" current of our times. Take, for example, this promotional blurb by the didge master Ash Dorgan: "World ambient trance music at its best. Cutting edge rhythms of didjeridu, carefully fused with a blend of world vocals and modern trance music, as never before recorded, to send you to transcendence." The didjshop.com Web site "sponsors a worldwide didjeridu meditation four times per year on the equinoxes and solstices at local sunset times." The site's text refers to the "deep reverence and caring for nature" of the Aboriginals, the sound that is "very relaxing and healing," and the instrument's power to help people "reconnect with nature, earth energy and each other." In these emerging social settings, the old romantic aura of folk music gains its most extravagant power to invoke magnetism in order to evoke affinity (and, in many cases, sales).

Folk music's authority to bond amateur musicians is not limited to borrowed sources and styles. A fine case study comes from Ruth Finnegan's 1980s comprehensive survey of musical groups in one English city, Milton Keynes. For folk music performers, she found, "their participation was a source of the greatest satisfaction," something they said "they spend more time thinking about than their work"; they "live for folk." Some of the activity is part of a national network, which harks back to the days of Cecil Sharp nearly a hundred years ago, but many groups are purely local. As with the Balkanites, Finnegan's folk enthusiasts are mostly professional and very well educated: "If any of the local music worlds could be regarded as 'middle class' it was that of folk music, for all that this ran so clearly counter to the image its practitioners wished to hold of themselves." Finnegan means here that the folk fans held strongly to the idea that they were involved in something old, oral, and pastoral, so downplayed their social status. But a strong ideological difference divides that sort of local purist from a more experimental wing, which continues what is itself a tradition: electric, folk, or folk-rock from the late 1960s and 1970s. The overlying attitudes and commitment, not the actual music, define the Milton Keynes scene: "There can be no real definition of local 'folk music' beyond saying that it was the kind of music played by those who called themselves 'folk' performers."

Some points jump out from the huge range of music making that folk music movements have generated. The seeds planted by early collectors, activists, and distributors continue to bear fruit decades or centuries later. People still identify strongly with the idea of an earlier age of rural, oral music, dance, and customs that can soothe and channel the anxiety and fatigue of today's multitasking and often alienated urbanites, whether those traditions come from close by or arrive from distant shores. The work of the folk music pioneers also lives on in the actual material: tunes, lyrics, dance steps, instrumental licks. No matter how much the founders filtered what they heard and notated through a system of standardization, it maintains an aura of authenticity for enthusiasts.

Groups reasonably untouched by all this mediation, such as urban immigrants, are still working out how to use the expressive resources that their parents or grandparents brought along from the countryside. They tend to generate new folk musics that build on collective memory as they celebrate occasions or resist social control. From their midst, stars are born from this communal energy. They add a new layer of mediation, between the home group and the larger world of the music marketplace. Stars can be a source of pride, as success stories, or of scorn, as "sell-outs." The boundaries of folk music remain flexible, defined from inside and outside groups, by many different types of social actors. All this activity works within a world of overarching, systematic structures, defined transnationally. A look at folk music today and in the future needs to consider that larger, global framework.

Chapter 6
Folk music today and tomorrow

Folk music frameworks

If there is a universal soundtrack to folk music today, it might be the
snapping of administrative umbrellas over the heads of musicians,
as part of the new international system. A music scene might look
up and see coverage constantly expanding, unfurled by a whole
group of agents: local and national tourism developers, music
marketers with far-flung networks, small-scale nongovernmental
organizations (NGOs), UNESCO, the World Intellectual Property
Organization (WIPO)…the list grows and grows. No easy
summary can describe all this bustling energy around the idea
of concepts such as "intangible cultural heritage," "safeguarding,"
and "sustainable economies"; endless events—annual world-
music expositions, the ever-increasing number of festivals; and
the proliferation of Internet ways of documenting, selling, and
displaying the visible and audible traces that musicians leave. A
short survey of three basic categories of umbrella activities sketches
an emerging framework for much twenty-first-century folk music.

The circuit

In the highly organized space of North America, as in other
Western countries, folk music thrives as nodes along a stratified
circuit of places and events. There are nearly five hundred

festivals in the United States and one hundred in Canada every year. At these group celebrations, professionals and amateurs mix. Significant coordination comes from the Folk Alliance (FA), started in 1989, with its three thousand professional members and this mission statement: "To strengthen and advance organizational and individual initiatives in folk music and dance through education, networking, advocacy, and professional and field development." The FA's annual meeting features five hundred juried and unofficial showcases, awards shows, workshops, and all the other strategies an organization can invent to attract and train members to go out into the wide world to sing and play their hearts out for the circuit's consumers. But the FA is not just for musicians: "Our community has grown to include record companies, publishers, presenters, agents, managers, music support services, manufacturers and artists that work in the folk world." Should this support system not be magnetic enough, the FA also offers benefits, from health insurance to car-rental discounts. It's a long way from earlier circuits, such as Woody Guthrie's dustbowl odyssey and Pete Seeger's union halls.

The circuit both creates and sustains what Thomas Gruning calls the "folk microindustry." At every level, standards of selection ensure "quality control:" "When Barker (a house concert booking agent) auditions performers he uses a printed form on which he grades such criteria as guitar style, use of imagery and rhyme, vocal range, use of humor, audience rapport, overall appearance, and a six-tiered cumulative rating." Would Blind Lemon Jefferson or Aunt Molly Jackson have survived this test? Given the fact that two-thirds of festivals feature "contemporary singer/songwriters" and that "the American folk landscape is not exactly brimming with dark faces," the circuit, as well as its audiences, does not seem to mirror the makeup of the general U.S. population. To compensate for this monochromatic scene, the circuit increasingly invites outside entertainment, from African to Celtic to the didjeridu, "creating a sense of sonic hybridity" for a "homogeneous audience."

But what does the circuit mean by "folk music" anyway? Maybe it's about a sense of lineage, from the revival era of the 1950s or the early recordings, and that is probably true for many players and listeners. But among the professionals, Gruning found that listening to the Beatles was a much more formative childhood musical experience than early familiarity with any of the iconic figures of the folk movement. Given this mainstream orientation, the general idea of folk music boils down to this summary: "Acoustic instruments that can be heard by everybody within earshot, a certain musical simplicity, and accessible, thoughtful, understandable lyrics are the most commonly quoted reasons for interest in contemporary folk music."

Gruning's description is not the last word on why and how folk music continues in active circulation; other countries, in Europe and elsewhere, have very different circuits, and even in the United States, a recent upsurge in college student interest in older styles seems less competitive, commercial, or dependent on popular music. At Wesleyan University, Abigail Washburn attracts an excited crowd, partly because she's connected to current folk icon Bela Fleck, but also because she travels to China and writes songs in Chinese. The opening to the "exotic" need not be about compensation for whiteness, in Gruning's terms, but it can perhaps signal a greater openness to musical exchange, beyond the level of the world-music or concert-hall fascination with the musical Other. On her 2008 blog from China, Washburn describes working with and writing songs about Sichuan earthquake victims. She sounds like an ethnomusicologist when she searches for "an intimate view of the evolution of art and tradition in the midst of enormous economic and social changes here."

Empathetic global outreach is not new to the folk-music movement. The Weavers, the legendary band with Pete Seeger that shaped the 1950s folk revival, put out a songbook full of "international" folk songs, including sources such as Indonesia, as part of leftist solidarity with working people everywhere. But they were not the first to listen to far-off voices. They were building on the somewhat different inclusive ideology of nineteenth-century American songbooks, which might even feature a Chinese item, as a distant antecedent to the Weavers and Abigail Washburn.

Beyond inquisitive individuals, the global circuit has become extremely formalized, even at a level of commercialism that is much lower than popular music's economic base. World Music Expo (WOMEX), a "world music support and development group" runs an annual event at different locations in Europe, which has attracted nearly five thousand companies and more than ten thousand delegates since 1994. WOMEX combines standardization and professionalization with talent development and outreach to take some of the strategies behind the Folk Alliance to a much broader audience. The organization blends very diverse ingredients for its successful recipe. Its annual award is given for any or all of these qualities: "musical excellence, social importance, commercial success, political impact, and lifetime achievement." Its head, Gerald Seligman, is a busy man who "participates in conferences and consults with governments [and] NGOs and at workshops throughout the world. As a Grammy-nominated producer he has created or compiled over 120 releases."

Perhaps looking for an image of social responsibility but also tapping into a different market, WOMEX has added an education category to its award. Here WOMEX overlaps with the outreach work of universities and music schools on the one hand and the educational work of commercial organizations such as the Grammy Foundation on the other. Circuits have a way of intersecting.

The system

Folk music's current pathways bring it to the crossroads of another set of national and international networks: what I call the System, a dense layer of "official" transnational organizations that have increasing influence. Two major players in this game are UNESCO and WIPO, made up of bureaucrats and lawyers. Both indulge in high-flown rhetoric about "safeguarding" and "protecting" traditional music, in differing ways.

For UNESCO, the operative term is "intangible cultural heritage" (ICH), which it defined this way in 2003: "the practices, representations, expressions, as well as the knowledge and skills, that communities, groups and, in some cases, individuals recognize as part of their cultural heritage." They go on to specify how ICH works: "Transmitted from generation to generation, [it] is constantly re-created by communities and groups in response to their environment, their interaction with nature and their history, and provides them with a sense of identity and continuity, thus promoting respect for cultural diversity and human creativity." ICH comes from the grassroots and offers communities something to hang on to, even if they can't look at it or hold it, the way you can the so-called tangible cultural heritage such as temples or pottery. It's a comforting picture of tradition as something agreed on that somehow demands respect, even though examples such as wartime Yugoslavia show that a common heritage can be split apart and engender contempt."

But who is "the community," and do people today keep transmitting from generation to generation? UNESCO is not sure, conceding that "communities have an open character, that they can be dominant or non-dominant, that they are not necessarily linked to specific territories and that one person can very well belong to different communities and switch communities.... It is difficult to use the term authentic in relation to ICH; some experts advise against its use in relation to living heritage." One way UNESCO gets around the problem it has created for itself is to make an official canon, in this case a list of "Masterpieces of the Oral and Intangible Heritage." By standardizing the world's musical traditions, UNESCO aims at helping them to achieve visibility and continuity: 90 of these Masterpieces from 107 different countries have been proclaimed over the last few years. This is ambition at a level on which only the System can operate.

On the ground, who actually directs the work of ICH and how it should be safeguarded by means of sustainable development? Usually it is not the community itself, but rather a kind of government, since UNESCO's basic work unit is a "state-party" who signs on to an international convention. The System can jump-start national energies, as in China's 2007 initiative to host a UNESCO meeting in the city of Chengdu, sponsor a huge international festival in the new ICH Park there, charter local and provincial research and protection teams, and open a National ICH Center. Friction can arise at many operational levels; international and local ideologies may well diverge; those safeguarding and sustainable goals may conflict. Is it social cohesion or economic development that comes first? ICH promises to influence the future development of folk music's evolution in all ways and many places as part of the System's power to make a difference in local life.

If they do manage to produce tangible products of the intangible heritage, musicians run headlong into WIPO, charged with supervising the world's intellectual property. Folk music is both unprotected and raided as globalization expands its marketplace reach. Coming from a different direction than UNESCO, WIPO aims to look out for local musicians' interests, both in terms of safeguarding rights and suggesting development goals. Two cases from Africa suggest the range of rhetoric. For the Aka Pygmies of Central Africa, UNESCO proposes to make an inventory of their music, then organize a festival of Aka Pygmy music and dance, and then move on to training seminars, which will prepare for radio and national television programs. The point is to "sensitize" the non-Pygmy population, enrich national identity, and, ultimately, encourage "cultural dialogue and the cultural integration of the Aka Pygmies in subregional Central Africa." This is the System moving in on local cultural politics, with music as the entry wedge.

Meanwhile, in Kenya, WIPO, like UNESCO, also worries about the effects of a multi-ethnic population, but from a very different angle: that of marketing. From their Web site: "Paradoxically, the very diversity of Kenya's musical scene represents a key challenge to developing a sustainable industry. In particular, its linguistic diversity has fragmented the market and made it more difficult for artists to develop unique and recognizable sounds that can serve as currency for access to mainstream global markets." Here, diversity is an obstacle, not a goal, for local music. The organization thinks training and copyright control could help to overcome an inefficient Kenyan music industry.

Like parallel railroad tracks, UNESCO and WIPO appear to—and might even—meet at the horizon as they converge on local musicians, formats, repertoires, styles, venues, performance, recording, distribution, patronage, and rewards. Whether this creates a musical train wreck is an open question. But the fact that the System increasingly influences the future and fate of folk music cannot be avoided.

The tourist

The world is awash in cultural tourists, people who leave their homes in search of diversion. In response, local communities and agencies prepare their own homes for the visitors. Sometimes, tourists go to a place just for the music, as in the case of pilgrimages to Graceland, Elvis's mansion in Tennessee, or to Bayreuth in Germany for Wagner operas, New Orleans for jazz, and Liverpool, with its Beatles shrines. But most curious travelers simply encounter music as part of the overall experience of being in a colorful place—an island stopover in a cruise, for example. Folk music appears as local color right at the hotel, often with performers in costumes, occasionally including bare-shirted men and scantily clad women to complete the time-worn equation of exotic = erotic. Musical tourism offers that sustainable development for many communities, from Africa to England.

Little of the writing on this topic digs into the response of the tourists themselves, but some of the literature illuminates the strategies and agendas of the locals. For the much-visited European island of Sardinia, Ignazio Macchiarella reports that amateur musicians produce a standardized show for tourists, then retire to a nearby bar, poke fun at the visitors, and sing the folk songs that they think of as their "real" heritage. On Bali, the population has interacted with Western tourists since the 1920s, so the story is well documented. It all started with intellectuals and bohemian artists whose fascination with the island led to long residences, unusual for tourism. One, by the name of Walter Spies, worked with the Balinese to alter a local ritual to make it striking for visitors. The monkey-chorus chant taken from mythology, *kecak*, remains the trademark of Bali to this day, even appearing in the films of Fellini and the Coen brothers as an ominous soundtrack to violence. So Westerners, in blending in with the Balinese, have operated as both tourists and cultural agents.

From the 1970s on, as jet-age tourism mushroomed, the Balinese began to realize that they had to have their own vision of sustainability. Evolving entertainment at the hotels and arranging for short tours of selected villages, the Balinese have drawn musical boundaries that keep local ceremonies and styles off-limits to foreigners. Sometimes, tourism seems as if it is eroding and displacing folk music in favor of altered formats, but local planning can make sure that people both cater to the cash cow of tourism *and* keep their culture, all through canny compartmentalization.

This is not an easy process, particularly when the waves of tourists crashing into your home are your fellow-citizens, rather than wandering Westerners. In the southern Chinese province of Yunnan, most visitors are from the majority Han group, coming to see the "exotic" minority peoples who live in the south. To support tourism for the Mosuo people, developers stress the role of women and nature—a popular enough pairing in travel promotion and one in line with Chinese attitudes about the region. Singing by a picturesque lakeside illustrates the theme nicely. As a promotional video puts it, "walking into the Mosuo is like walking into a romantic lake and singing-dancing sea." In Malaysia, an even more complex strategy of entertaining domestic tourists evolved among Eurasians who needed an identity after the British left the country in the 1950s. They took their musical cue from the first colonial power, Portugal, and invented a village for visitors where they successfully performed a new repertoire of "old" Portuguese folk music. These Eurasians became what Margaret Sarkissian calls "cultural chameleons," who offered "a ready-made 'tradition' that was recognizably European"— hence exotic for Malaysians—"but not British."

8. The *Mosuo Qing* performance center in southeastern China was built for tourism, with a poster advertising the folk music ensemble.

Tourism is indeed the mother of musical invention. It makes a real contribution to any group's drive for distinctiveness as a partner in what John and Jean Comaroff have termed "Ethnicity, Inc.," a worldwide trend for self-definition arising out of mixed motivations, any of which might involve the folk music sensibility. The future of folk music research lies partly in finding the overlaps and differences between people's internal self-definition and the frameworks devised and promoted by the System, from the UN and WIPO to thousands of activist NGOs. The tourists operate as both consumers and transmitters of the resulting mix.

Folk music futures: on the move

Just as the pace of change picked up when country dwellers turned into urban immigrants, so the recent upsurge in people moving across borders keeps musicians on the move, but in new

9. The highly costumed and choreographed performance for the *Gemugua* festival of the Mosuo people, southeastern China.

and sometimes uncharted ways. Migrant workers, refugees, and diasporic populations scatter from home in increasingly large numbers, with complex musical results. Diaspora, the idea of how people live away from a present or past homeland, has been looked at the most intensively, but the more closely you examine the situation, the less simple it gets. Working on the musical experience of people separated from their place of origin, researchers now "suggest that rather than focus on diaspora as a dislocation we start from an alternative premise: that diaspora can be the space in which people establish 'home.'" This quote is from Tina Ramnarine, who has looked at Caribbean populations that have settled into life in Trinidad, Toronto, New York, and London. Everywhere, "music has provided the soundtracks for daily life, offering a shield against harsh work conditions and evoking memories of people and places elsewhere." But that "elsewhere" is multiple: "the musical expressions of the Caribbean look to various diasporas, showing us how one diaspora interacts and overlaps with another...how diasporic identities are shifted and transformed, and how one person can hold several diasporic identities—as African or Indian or Jamaican or Cuban or Caribbean," all of this happening simultaneously in many countries, which are often closely in touch.

Ramnarine flags a telling moment of musical assertiveness among tempest-tossed people settling on several shores: the claim by the members of the Association of British Calypsonians "that calypso in Britain should be recognized as being 'British folk music.'" Calypso is a form that most world-music consumers would identify as purely Caribbean, particularly Trinidadian. It began as folk music on that island in the early 1900s and often projected anticolonial sentiments. But through the record industry, calypso entered the living rooms and dance halls of non-Caribbean people worldwide. So how could it be "British folk music?" She suggests that this bold assertion is a provocation, flying in the face of Cecil Sharp's drive for "English songs for Englishmen." The British Calypsonians are insisting that they too can shape national music in Britain, which they have done over several generations by now, so why not call it folk music?

Even very locally grounded events, such as huge annual festivals, represent music that is both diasporic and national. Ramnarine points out that the crowded and popular Caribana Toronto creates a space and time for Caribbean people, living abroad, to develop their expressive culture and link up with the histories and contemporary culture of groups like themselves that live in other places, including Britain, the United States, and the Caribbean. They are representing and developing their culture on the move, both to outsiders—thousands of tourists yielding millions of dollars—and to themselves, brandishing ever-changing folk music in ways that defy easy analysis. The future of this folk music belongs to people who think outside older frameworks of identity.

Another multiple-diaspora music that challenges clichés is "klezmer," a single, summary word for a scene based on eastern European Jewish roots music, revitalized since the 1970s. It all began around 1900, when the musicians of Yiddish-speaking culture, called *klezmer*, participated in the mass migration of one Jewish diaspora, in the Russian Empire, Romania, and Poland, to another, largely in the United States. There was no "klezmer music," since, as true professional folk performers, klezmers would play anything an audience asked for. But as these versatile instrumentalists assimilated to mainstream American styles, much of the older European music faded. In the 1970s it was re-energized by a young, roots-seeking generation of Jewish American musicians. They channeled tunes, mostly from old commercial recordings but also from surviving artists, into concert halls and recording studios, first in the United States and then in Europe, including countries such as Germany and Italy, where the earlier music had never really circulated in the "old days."

As non-Jews have joined the klezmer scene, the repertoire and approach have evolved from a folk music to a world-music profile in many ways, yet the community spirit still survives that will allow klezmer to survive the fashion trends of the circuit. You can find the music and its sensibility thriving in Germany, where it bears the ambivalence of audiences who know in the back of their minds that Germans annihilated the music in the Holocaust. Klezmer has proven to be useful in teaching that sad story to young Germans; one report says that the songs and tunes do a better job of Holocaust education than the usual pedagogical devices. The Yiddish language is close enough to German so that listeners can identify. In Russia and Ukraine, klezmer has made a significant comeback of late, appealing to a now-nostalgic population of Jews. Back in the United States, the same stylings can propel a wedding at a synagogue as "heritage" music for an audience two or three generations removed from eastern Europe.

In all these sites, past folk music becomes an important part of future structures of feeling, among very different populations, who perhaps do not share direct descent from the musicians who started moving the tunes across geographic and conceptual borders. There are limits; klezmer can never be noticed by the System, since there's no "indigenous" population in a nation-state that can claim it as intangible cultural heritage in an officially recognized way.

At home

Folk music travels freely and widely in all kinds of global networks, but it also stays at home. While these patterns are not mutually exclusive—scholars have coined the term "glocal" for the way local music fits into the global context—not every place is just a neighborhood in the global village, and not all musicians are just wannabe world-music stars.

Southeastern Europe is a place that remains regional in many ways. This has something to do with very old histories. For centuries, the area was under the sway of the Turkish-led Ottoman Empire, so musical pathways and resemblances can always be re-energized, given the right conditions. Then there's the European Union, to which, as the West makes sure, the Balkan nations always feel themselves peripheral. The description earlier of musical dissonance and belligerence, following the collapse of Yugoslavia, still holds true to some extent. Yet recently, older connections shine through, as Donna Buchanan says: "Musicians are making that case that 'Balkan' as a place, subjectivity, and aesthetic sensibility can and should be celebrated for both its many remarkable inherent commonalities and its equally abundant, intriguing, and captivating differences.... Beginning in the 1990s, increasingly sophisticated musical productions are being marketed chiefly for domestic, regional consumption rather than distribution by powerful international media giants."

If this can happen in a place so marked by political violence, the chances of other world areas thinking regionally, rather than nationally, look good, despite the workings of the circuit and the System. Of course, the actual content of music called "folk" will shift: "In the former Yugoslav territories the adjective *narodna* [folk], which once referred to rural traditional music, now often points to pop-folk, whereas *ethno* [ethno] has become the word of choice to describe rural roots musics of the type valued by intellectuals and specialized audiences," as Svanibor Pettan remarks.

In some places, whole communities keep right on singing and playing for their own benefit, even when they are in contact with other musics. The Q'eros people of Peru are one example, well documented by Holly Wissler, who has been collaborating with them for years. They live on three levels in the Andes, low, medium, and high (4,000 meters/13,000 feet), depending on what they can grow when and where their animals thrive seasonally. They also take ritual journeys, often grueling, to support their faith. The Q'eros say that music helps them to survive: "without singing, we would walk in silence, like ghosts." Every man makes his own flute to accompany women's singing.

Songs and flute tunes provide continuity with the landscape, the animals, and both personal and group narratives. People sing individual improvised laments for the loss of loved ones. Even when not mourning, "all of a sudden, when we are singing, the heart feels sadness. Grief comes." But they also say: "we cry from happiness; we cry from grief and joy." Folk music runs deep for the Q'eros.

This is not an idyllic lifestyle—the work and weather are grueling. Nor is it an enclosed environment. Sometimes the Q'eros walk a day to get to the city of Cusco, where they play for tourists. They also pick up the music of urban immigrants. Some young people bring back city styles to enrich their regular repertoire: "we learned to play by listening to cassette tapes and the radio." They also gather songs and dances from the other pilgrims who join them on the annual Qoyur Rita pilgrimage to high glaciers. And there's a chance a highway might run closer to their homes, so they say "if the road arrives, I think our songs will be lost." But for the moment, the Q'eros still get together annually to choose this year's song, which will be sung constantly around the annual carnival season, perhaps in praise of a particular mountain flower. Time is not on the side of this type of local folk music, but it survives.

Yet even in a crowded, multi-ethnic society, a small group of eloquent musicians can keep their traditions strong. Music might even give them an enviable reputation among their neighbors. The Sambla of Burkina Faso, described by Julie Strand, are just one of a set of ethnic groups in a part of west Africa where xylophone playing is common enough. But here they stand out, as surrounding people concede that the Sambla sound is exceptionally virtuosic and expressive. In their villages, children simply pick up instrumental skills by watching and, finally, joining ensembles, the way musicians in folk societies worldwide have always done. True, they do hear popular music from elsewhere, but it doesn't change their music system.

The urge to maintain handmade, homespun sounds never really disappears. It will increasingly become entangled in the networks of the circuit, the System, and the tourist. No one can say which direction musical minds will move, but the urge to honor memory, make a mark as an expressive member of your group—however defined—and to keep it local will allow folk music to carry on across space and time.

References

Chapter 1

Judith Becker, "Ethnomusicology and Empiricism in the Twenty-First Century, *Ethnomusicology* 53, no. 3 (Fall 2009): 478–501.

Ciaran Carson, *Last Night's Fun: In and Out of Time with Irish Music* (New York: North Point Press, 1996).

Eric Charry, *Mande Music* (University of Chicago Press, 2000).

Steven Feld, *Sound and Sentiment* (Philadelphia: University of Pennsylvania Press, 1982).

Henry Glassie, *Passing the Time in Balleymenone* (Bloomington: Indiana University Press, 1995).

I. Kiss, *Lakodalom* (Budapest: Hungarian Academy of Sciences, 1956).

Ted Levin, *Where Rivers and Mountains Sing* (Bloomington: Indiana University Press, 2006).

Bernard Lortat-Jacob, *Sardinian Chronicles* (Chicago: University of Chicago Press, 1995).

Tullia Magrini, "Women's 'Work of Pain' in Christian Mediterranean Europe," *Music and Anthropology* 3 (1998), available at http://research.umbc.edu/eol/MA/index/number3/ma_ind3.htm.

Marina Roseman, *Healing Sounds from the Malaysian Rainforest* (Berkeley: University of California Press, 1991).

Julie Strand, *The Sambla Xylophone: Tradition and Identity in Burkina Faso* (PhD diss., Wesleyan University, 2009).

Sean Williams and Lillis Ó Laoire, *Bright Star of the West: Joe Heaney, Irish Song-Man* (New York: Oxford University Press, 2010).

Richard Wolf, *The Black Cow's Footprint: Time, Space, and Music in the Lives of the Kotas of South India* (Urbana: University of Illinois Press, 2006).

Hugo Zemp, "Aspects of 'Are'are Musical Theory," *Ethnomusicology* 23, no. 1 (Jan. 1979): 5–48.

Chapter 2

D. M. Balashov and Lu Kraskovskaia, *Russkie svadebnye pesni Terskogo berega Belogo moria* (Leningrad: Muzyka, 1969).

Tristram Potter Coffin and Roger deV. Renwick, *The British Traditional Ballad in North America* (Austin: University of Texas Press, 1977).

Dorothea Hast and Stanley Scott, *Music in Ireland: Experiencing Music, Expressing Culture* (New York: Oxford University Press, 2004).

Debora Kodish, "Absent Gender, Silent Encounter," *Journal of American Folklore* 100 (1987): 573–78.

Chana Mlotek and Mark Slobin, eds. *Yiddish Folksongs from the Ruth Rubin Archive* (Detroit: Wayne State University Press, 2007).

Carol Muller, *Focus: Music of South Africa*, 2nd ed. (New York: Routledge, 2008).

Ankica Petrović, "Perceptions of Ganga," http://www.imota.net/html/ankica_petroviae.html, accessed January 2009.

Suzel Reily, *Voices of the Magi: Enchanted Journeys in Southeast Brazil* (Chicago: University of Chicago Press, 2002).

Anthony Seeger, *Why Suya Sing: A Musical Anthropology of an Amazonian People* (Cambridge: Cambridge University Press, 1987).

Carol Silverman, *Romani Routes: Cultural Politics and Balkan Romani Music in Diaspora* (New York: Oxford University Press, 2011).

Chapter 3

Donna Buchanan, *Performing Democracy: Bulgarian Music and Musicians in Transition* (Chicago: University of Chicago Press, 2006).

Dorothea Hast and Stanley Scott, *Music in Ireland: Experiencing Music, Expressing Culture* (New York: Oxford University Press, 2004).

Richard Kurin, "Why We Do the Festival," brochure for the 1989 Festival of American Folklife (Washington, DC: Smithsonian Institution, 1989).

James Leary, *Polkabilly: How the Goose Island Ramblers Redefined American Folk Music* (New York: Oxford University Press, 2006).

Aaron Paige, *Subaltern Sounds: Fashioning Folk Music in Tamil Nadu* (master's thesis, Wesleyan University, 2009).

Michael Pisani, *Imagining Native America in Music* (New Haven, CT: Yale University Press, 2005).

Martin Stokes, *The Arabesk Debate: Music and Musicians in Modern Turkey* (Oxford: Clarendon Press, 1992).

Chapter 4

Erika Brady, *A Spiral Way: How the Phonograph Changed Ethnography* (Jackson: University of Mississippi Press, 1999).

Donna Buchanan, *Performing Democracy: Bulgarian Music and Musicians in Transition* (Chicago: University of Chicago Press, 2006).

Beverly Diamond, "Overview of Music in Canada," in *The Garland Encyclopedia of World Music*, ed. Ellen Koskoff, 3:1066–1100 (London: Routledge, 2001).

Bob Dylan, *Chronicles* (New York: Simon & Schuster, 2005).

Steven Feld, "Pygmy Pop: A Genealogy of Schizophonic Mimesis," *Yearbook for Traditional Music* 28 (1996), 1–35.

Charlotte Frisbie, "American Indian Musical Repatriation," in Koskoff, *Garland Encyclopedia of World Music*, 3:491–504.

Chris Goertzen, *Fiddling for Norway: Revival and Identity* (Chicago: University of Chicago Press, 1997).

Richard Kurin, "Why We Do the Festival," *Smithsonian Folklife Festival* (Washington, DC: Smithsonian Institution, 1985).

James Leary, *Polkabilly: How the Goose Island Ramblers Redefined American Folk Music* (New York: Oxford University Press, 2006).

Guy Logsdon, Liner notes for *Buffalo Skinners: Woody Guthrie, the Asch Recordings*, vol. 4. Smithsonian Folkways Records LC9628, 1999.

Allan Marett, *Songs, Dreaming, and Ghosts: The Wangga of North Australia* (Middletown, CT: Wesleyan University Press, 2005).

Mukurtu. http://demo.mukurtuarchive.org/help.php?topic=2, accessed 2009.

Aaron Paige, *Subaltern Sounds: Fashioning Folk Music in Tamil Nadu* (master's thesis, Wesleyan University, 2009).

Anthony Seeger, "Theories Forged in the Crucible of Action: The Joys, Dangers, and Potentials of Advocacy and Fieldwork," in *Shadows in the Field*, 2nd ed., ed. Gregory F. Barz and Timothy J. Cooley (New York: Oxford University Press, 2008).

Richard Spottswood, "Commercial Ethnic Recordings in the United States," in *Ethnic Recordings in America: A Neglected Heritage*, Studies in American Folklife, no. 1: 51–66 (Washington, DC: Library of Congress, 1982).

Martin Stokes, *The Arabesk Debate: Music and Musicians in Modern Turkey* (Oxford: Clarendon Press, 1992).

Chapter 5

Eric Charry, "Introduction," in Babatunde Olatunji, *The Beat of My Drum*, 1–19 (Philadelphia: Temple University Press, 2005).

Ruth Finnegan, *The Hidden Musicians: Music-Making in an English Town* (Middletown, CT: Wesleyan University Press, 2007 [1989]).

Lawrence Foana'ota, "Panpipes in the Solomon Islands," concert brochure, 2006.

Philip S. Foner, *American Labor Songs of the Nineteenth Century* (Champaign: University of Illinois Press, 1975).

Peter Hadley, *The Didjeridu Dispersion: The Transmission and Transformation of a Hollow Log* (PhD diss., Wesleyan University, 2007).

Deborah Kapchan, *Traveling Spirit Masters: Moroccan Gnawa Trance and Music in the Global Marketplace* (Middletown, CT: Wesleyan University Press, 2007).

Lois Kuter, "Celtic Music," in *The Garland Encyclopedia of World Music: Europe*, ed. Timothy Rice, James Porter, and Chris Goertzen, 8:319–23 (London: Routledge, 2000).

Mirjana Lausević, *Balkan Fascination: Creating an Alternative Music Culture in America* (New York: Oxford University Press, 2007).

Mirjana Lausević, "The *Ilahiya* as a Symbol of Bosnian Muslim National Identity," in *Retuning Culture,* ed. M. Slobin, 117–35 (Durham, NC: Duke University Press, 1996).

Carol Muller, *Focus: Music of South Africa*, 2nd ed. (New York: Routledge, 2008).

Babtunde Olatunji, *The Beat of My Drum* (Philadelphia: Temple University Press, 2005).

Ljerka Vidić Rasmussen, *Newly Composed Folk Music of Yugoslavia* (London: Routledge, 2002).

Pete Seeger, introductory notes to *The Original Talking Union & Other Union Songs with the Almanac Singers*, Folkways Records FP85-1, 1955.

Carol Silverman, *Romani Routes: Cultural Politics and Balkan Romani Music in Diaspora* (New York: Oxford University Press, 2011).

Graeme Smith, "Celtic Australia: Bush Bands, Irish Music, Folk Music, and the New Nationalism," in *Celtic Modern: Music at the Global Fringe*, ed. M. Stokes and P. Bohlman, 73–91 (Lanham, MD: Scarecrow Press, 2003).

Martin Stokes, "Introduction," in Stokes and Bohlman, *Celtic Modern*.

Thomas Turino, *Moving Away from Silence: Music of the Peruvian Altiplan and the Experience of Urban Migration* (Chicago: University of Chicago Press, 1993).

Christopher Waterman, *Juju: A Social History and Ethnography of an African Popular Music* (Chicago: University of Chicago Press, 1990).

Desi Wilkinson, "'Celtitude,' Professionalism, and the *Fest Noz* in Traditional Music in Brittany," in Stokes and Bohlman, *Celtic Modern*, 219–56.

Chapter 6

Michael Bakan, "The Abduction of the Signifying Monkey Chant: Schizophonic Transmogrifications of Balinese *Kecak* in Fellini's *Satyricon* and the Coen Brothers' *Blood Simple*," *Ethnomusicology Forum* 18, no. 1 (2009): 83–106.

Donna Buchanan, *Balkan Popular Culture and the Ottoman Ecumene* (Lanham, MD: Scarecrow Press, 2007).

Carol Croella, "On the Beat—Tapping the Potential of Kenya's Music Industry," http://www.wipo.int/wipo_magazine/en/2007/04/article_0001.html.

Thomas R. Gruning, *Millenium Folk: American Folk Music Since the Sixties* (Athens: University of Georgia Press, 2006).

Svanibor Pettan, *Rom Musicians in Kosovo: Interaction and Creativity* (Budapest: Institute for Musicology of the Hungarian Academy for Sciences, 2002).

Tina Ramnarine, *Beautiful Cosmos: Performance and Belonging in the Caribbean Diaspora* (London: Pluto Press, 2007).

Margaret Sarkissian, "Cultural Chameleons: Portuguese Eurasian Strategies for Survival in Post-Colonial Malaysia," *Journal of Southeast Asian Studies* 28, no. 2 (1997): 249–62.

Julie Strand, *The Sambla Xylophone: Tradition and Identity in Burkina Faso* (PhD diss., Wesleyan University, 2009).

Holly Wissler, *Kusisqa Waqashayu: From Grief and Joy We Sing,* documentary film, 2009.

Folk Music

Further reading

Internet resources

www.oxfordmusiconline.com/public/book/omo_gmo

Offers the *Grove Dictionary of Music*, also available at libraries. Most comprehensive English-language music encyclopedia.

http://glnd.alexanderstreet.com

Has the *Garland Encyclopedia of World Music*, in ten volumes. Splendid, comprehensive source for short accounts of musics of the world.

www.folklife.si.edu

Site for the Smithsonian Center for Folklife and Cultural Heritage, which includes video from the annual Folklife Festival in Washington, D.C., among other helpful links for U.S. and world folk music.

www.loc.gov/folklife/onlinecollections.html

Contains a number of listenable archives of holdings of the American Folklife Center of the Library of Congress, including fiddle tunes and Native American music.

www.folkways.si.edu

Site of Smithsonian Folkways Records, which allows you to browse, sample, and purchase the entire vast catalogue of the label, dating back to the 1940s, including video clips.

www.folkways.si.edu/projects_initiatives/global_sound.aspx

Includes Folkways music as well as access to other archives of folk music in places such as India and Africa.

http://www.indiana.edu/~libarchm/

Archives of Traditional Music at Indiana University, "the largest university-based ethnographic sound archives in the United States."

www.phonogrammarchiv.at/wwwnew

Searchable site of the Phonogrammarchiv, a major sound archive in Vienna.

www.folkstreams.net

A treasure trove of older (back to 1960s) documentary films on folk music, mainly in the United States, many with significant commentary.

www.folkalliance.org

The home of Folk Alliance, an organization of presenters and artists that promotes the folk music circuit in the United States and elsewhere.

www.womex.org

The home of WOMEX, which schedules annual conferences to promote world music; the site has clips and information.

http://afghanistan.wesleyan.edu

Mark Slobin's multimedia Web site with many of the materials of his 1967–72 fieldwork in northern Afghanistan, including pdf files of his entire book.

www.nativedrums.ca

Site devoted to First Nations culture and music in Canada, with a companion Web site on native dance, www.nativedance.ca.

www.wesleyan.edu/music/vim

The Virtual Instrument Museum, based on Wesleyan University's collection of worldwide musical instruments.

www.mdw.ac.at/ive/en/index.html

Site for Vienna's Institut für Volksmusikforschung (Institute for Folk Music Research and Ethnomusicology); research and publication hub, English text available.

www.culturalequity.org

Site for the archive of Alan Lomax, pioneering ethnomusicologist and folk music promoter, whose recorded folk music work is appearing serially with extensive new annotation on Rounder Records as the Alan Lomax Collection.

www.woodyguthrie.org

Site of the Woody Guthrie Foundation.

www.pearl.arts.ed.ac.uk

Site of the server for the School of Scottish Studies, with downloadable content.

http://visarkiv.se

Site of the Swedish Center for Folk Music and Jazz Studies. Publications on folk music are readable in pdf format.

www.itma.ie/English/Introduction.html

Site of the Irish Traditional Music Archive.

www.patchworkproductions.org

Contains video clips of traditional Bulgarian music performance.

Books

Abu-Lughod, Lila. *Veiled Sentiments: Honor and Poetry in a Bedouin Society*. Berkeley: University of California Press, 1999.

Berliner, Paul. *The Soul of Mbira: Music and Traditions of the Shona People of Zimbabwe*. Chicago: University of Chicago Press, 1993.

Bronson, Bertrand. *Traditional Tunes of the Child Ballads*. Berkeley: University of California Press, 1952.

Child, Francis James. *The English and Scottish Popular Ballads*. Mineola, NY: Dover, 2003 [1965].

Cohen, Norman. *Long Steel Rail: The Railroad in American Folksong*. Urbana: University of Illinois Press, 2000.

Cohen, Ronald, ed. *Alan Lomax: Selected Writings, 1934–1997*. New York: Routledge, 2003.

Cooley, Timothy. *Making Music in the Polish Tatras: Tourists, Ethnographers, and Mountain Musicians*. Bloomington: Indiana University Press, 2005.

Cowdery, James. *The Melodic Tradition of Ireland*. 2nd ed. Kent, OH: Kent State University Press, 2008.

Filene, Benjamin. *Romancing the Folk: Public Memory and American Roots Music*. Chapel Hill: University of North Carolina Press, 2000.

Hesselink, Nathan. *P'ungmul: South Korean Drumming and Dance*. Chicago: University of Chicago Press, 2006.

Hopkins, Pandora. *Aural Thinking in Norway: Performance and Communication with the Hardingfele*. New York: Human Sciences Press, 1986.

Lassiter, Luke E. *The Power of Kiowa Song*. Tucson: University of Arizona Press, 1998.

Levin, Theodore. *The Hundred Thousand Fools of God*. Bloomington: Indiana University Press, 1996.

——— . *Where Rivers and Mountains Sing: Sound, Music, and Nomadism in Tuva and Beyond*. Bloomington: Indiana University Press, 2006.

Lomax, Alan. *Selected Writings, 1934–1997*. Edited by Ronald Cohen. New York: Routledge, 2003.

McAlister, Elizabeth. *Rara: Vodou, Power, and Performance in Haiti*. Berkeley: University of California Press, 2002.

Miller, Rebecca. *Carriacou String Band Serenade: Performing Identity in the Eastern Caribbean*. Middletown CT: Wesleyan University Press, 2007.

Paredes, Americo. *With His Pistol in His Hand: A Border Ballad and Its Hero*. Austin: University of Texas Press, 1970.

Pellicer, Sergio Navarrete. *Maya Achi Marimba Music in Guatemala*. Philadelphia: Temple University Press, 2005.

Picken, Laurence. *Folk Musical Instruments of Turkey*. Oxford: Oxford University Press, 1975.

Rees, Helen. *Echoes of History: Naxi Music in Modern China*. New York: Oxford University Press, 2000.

Rice, Timothy. *Music in Bulgaria*. New York: Oxford University Press, 2004.

Rosenberg, Neil. *Transforming Tradition: Folk Music Revivals Examined.* Urbana: University of Illinois Press, 1993.

Seeger, Ruth Crawford. *The Music of American Folk Song.* Edited by L. Polonsky and J. Tick. Rochester, NY: University of Rochester Press, 2001.

Slobin, Mark. *Fiddler on the Move: Exploring the Klezmer World.* New York: Oxford University Press, 2000.

——. *Music in the Culture of Northern Afghanistan.* Tucson: University of Arizona Press, 1976. Available on pdf at http://afghanistan.wesleyan.edu.

——. *Old Jewish Folk Music: The Collections and Writings of Moshe Beregovski.* Syracuse, NY: Syracuse University Press, 2000.

Suchoff, Benjamin, ed. *Bela Bartok Essays.* Lincoln: University of Nebraska Press, 1992.

Sugarman, Jane. *Engendering Song: Singing and Subjectivity at Prespa Albanian Weddings.* Chicago: University of Chicago Press, 1997.

Sweers, Britta. *Electric Folk: The Changing Face of British Traditional Music.* New York: Oxford University Press, 2005.

Tang, Patricia. *Masters of the Sabar: Wolof Griot Percussionists of Senegal.* Philadelphia: Temple University Press, 2007.

Titon, Jeff. *Old-time Kentucky Fiddle Tunes.* Lexington: University Press of Kentucky, 2001.

——. *Powerhouse for God: Speech, Chant, and Song in an Appalachian Baptist Church.* Austin: University of Texas Press, 1988.

Vander, Judith. *Songprints: The Musical Experience of Five Shoshone Women.* Urbana: University of Illinois Press, 1988.

Wade, Bonnie C., and Patricia Sheehan Campbell. Global Music Series. New York: Oxford University Press, 2003. www.oup.com/us/catalog/general/?queryField=keyword&query=global+music+series&view=usa&viewVeritySearchResults=true.

Waterman, Christopher. *Juju: A Social History and Ethnography of an African Popular Music.* Chicago: University of Chicago Press, 1990.

Zheng, Su. *Claiming Diaspora: Music, Transnationalism, and Cultural Politics in Asian/Chinese America.* New York: Oxford University Press, 2010.

Index